MW00962307

FOR

My Mummy & her smile!

My Mamu & his never ending support

My Shamim Auntie & her prayers.

My brother, Ahraz, for being my biggest back up!

And Mr. Mushtaq Shiekh

For being the coolest boss in the world!

And Ashish Raikar

For telling me to write a book!

Copyright © Azhan, 2009

Published by

Expression publications

All rights reserved.

No part of this publication may be reproduced, stored in a retrieval system, or transmitted, in any form or by any means, electronic, mechanical, photocopying, recording or otherwise, without the prior permission of the publisher.

ISBN-978-81-905919-1-1

Dedicated to…

My father & grandfather with whom I was not able to talk as much I would have loved to......

1st

When the Mughal emperor Jehangir referred to Kashmir as the heaven on earth, I am pretty sure he had never been to this place. Nainital. For me, it has to be the heaven on earth. And when I die, I will tell my angels to make me a Nainital. A Nainital exclusively for me. Probably I will also allow ammi-abba to live with me. But I am in no doubt that they will order their angels the same. I don't know how far this holds true, or how far is this possible, at least abba always agreed, that if you live a pure life, stick to the laws of Islam, *this is possible.*

And that was the belief which used to make me more resolute as an eight year old, to visit the mosque five times a day, wash my little hands and feet rigorously, just before the *imam* would call in for the *namaaz.*

More resolute to wear my skull cap with pride on my head with the kurta and the pajama ending way above my navel, making sure that the bump of my ankle clearly shows in a typical maulvi fashion. Abba says it gets you *sawaab* and is a *sunnat.* The higher the *sunnat* in one's kitty, the higher are the chances of making it big in your afterlife.

More resolute to keep my *rozas*-fasts in the month of Ramadan sincerely. Unlike my madrasa friends who discreetly go to the tap in the *Bhootiya Mahal,* a derelict building behind the mosque and quench their thirst. They say there are many ugly and nasty *jinns* in there. But their urge to get a drop of water on their dry tongues and in their dehydrated bodies used to consume the fear of the *jinn.* I didn't do that since I desperately wanted my own Nainital.

And after every time I used to ascend after bowing down in front of the almighty, after I had kept my fast with the utmost honesty and dedication, the thought used to look very much plausible.

Wow! "My own Nainital!" The notion alone used to give me goose-bumps.

I along with my family used to visit this beautiful town, sitting pretty at the foot of the great Himalayas, every summer for a week's time. And it was always the most awaited week in the whole year for me. A month prior to my vacations, my inquisitive part would pester ammi asking the same question over and over again, 'when are we leaving?' Days used to pass, as if in a slow motion, making me more anxious and agitated.

Some very obnoxious stuff used to happen inside my tummy whenever my mind used to remind me of the pear shaped Naini lake, the pedal boats, the picturesque scene from the snow view point, for which one had to take a cable car. Tickets were 80 Rupees for ammi-abba, while for me they were 40. I remember the rates very well because abba used to bleat every time, 'I am paying 40 rupees to show you some white dust.'

Then there was the Cheena peak, from where one could not only see a broad swath of the snow clad high Himalaya, but also obtain a panoramic view of Nainital town itself. The summit was an invigorating hike from Nainital town. One had to walk a good couple of miles. For the less energetic visitors, ponies could be hired. Obviously we used to hire one, as we had with us one of the most indolent persons in the world. My abba.

Then there was a zoo, where I used to tease the tigers and the leopards, but they never reacted. They say leopards are the fastest animals on the planet. I don't agree. These tigers and leopards are the most lethargic bunch of animals who hardly move their asses. Some much naughtier kids in jeans and T-shirts used to throw pebbles at them as well, but they never, never moved. Just used to keep staring at us and wink their eyes as if they want to sleep and sleep some more. I have growled many times at them, 'Huaaaa.' Still no response.

According to me, monkeys or *langurs*, I don't know the difference between the two though, are the fastest creatures. Once out of the blue, one of them leapt out from a tree, bounced twice, snooped abba's skull cap and vanished in the bushes nearby. Abba stood there horror struck, while ammi laughed her lungs out. Her eyes were left red with tears by the time we reached our small hotel room. She later told about the incidence over a dozen times to our relatives.

The only place we used to skip from the itinerary was the Naina-Devi temple. I don't know why we never visited that temple. Only once we stood outside and watched people entering in herds and coming out in herds. I don't feel that we would have become impure like my abba suggested, just by stepping inside. Probably my abba was a little apprehensive of his attire and his never ending beard. These and many similar incidences used to send my rational wheels churning.

Apart from that, the hustle-bustle of the main market, the matches being played at the *'Flat,'* as the ground was called, the governor's house, and of course the horse riding sessions are all still very fresh in my memory. The last time we visited, riding had been prohibited inside the town. They said, a lot of fish are dying in the Naini lake and it's dangerous for the town's fragile ecosystem. Abba had muttered 'how are the death of fish in the lake and horse-riding related? Have you ever seen a horse feeding on a fish. Huh!'

I remember, that summer, along with the hill station we had planned to visit the Jim Corbett National park, famous for its tigers and huge tusker elephants. As it was very close to Nainital, the expenditure was not going to be that high. Abba had given the idea a nod after consulting a local guide a zillion times. The memories keep on getting vague with passing time, but I still remember the sanctuary quite well. It was full of trees, small lakes and then very small lakes. Ravines, ridges and small plateaus with varying aspects and degrees of slopes. Serene, peaceful, and as calm as a cow. We were to camp there for two days.

On the first evening our guide suddenly came yelling towards our tent, 'there is a python down the slope, gulping a fat mouse. Come one, come all. There is a python....' Eyes popping out of his sockets, hands going up and down, clapping, he was calling all the tourists camping there. More than the excitement of watching a python, the people were convinced by his frantic behavior. He was obviously a veteran at his job. I and ammi rushed to the spot. Abba followed lethargically. The python was lying majestically with prey in his mouth. I watched the whole process transfixed. The python was gradually, very slowly, at a snail's pace guzzling the mouse. It took almost an hour for him to take it in completely. I and ammi were the only ones watching it right till the end. It lay there still, like a lazy whore who has just been screwed. I could clearly see the paunch in his belly, exactly of the shape of a mouse. We were so gripped, we didn't notice that abba had already left. When we went back, he had puked all around our tent.

Ammi as usual cracked the same old joke on abba. 'Your name should read *Begum* Muqarram Jalal, and mine must be *Janaab* Najma Jalal. Just look at the way you have puked around.' With no obvious replies, abba sat there calmly chewing tobacco inadvertently.

The same night there was news that a tigress had ventured in the local village, broken the hut and taken a 5 year old girl.

Love, Lust & Lies

'Allah!' Was all that abba could utter, and I knew straightaway, we will be leaving with the first rays of sunlight next morning.

It is understood that we never, ever, on future trip of ours went to Corbett. Though I always wanted to go again, I never dared to put forward my idea.

I never had any complaints to make, even if we were going to the same place every year. However, my ammi had some. Once she got into a gruesome verbal duel with abba.

'How many times will we go to the same old place?'

Silence!

'Do you know there are many other hill stations in this world?'

Silence!

'If not in the world, I know of some in India. There is Shimla, Mount Abu, Kullu-Manali. Have you heard of them?'

Silence!

'You and your great silence! You are such a recluse.'

Silence!

My abba rarely retaliated. *'To respond is positive, but to react is negative.'* He told me this countless times. He had the same patience like those lazy leopards at the zoo.

Thanks to his great silence, as ammi used to put it in, our holiday location never moved. And for me, Nainital was the only known place in the world apart from my small house in my small town, and my small madrasa in my small mosque. This is one of the strong reasons why I have always been head over heels in love with this town. That was the only place I had *ever* been to and *always* been to for my vacations. Everything about Nainital simply used to delight me. I used to be filled with bliss.

Abba used to comment, 'Nainital is a place where you can live and die peacefully, gladly, and contentedly. The crisp and fresh breeze of this valley will take you straight to the doorsteps of *jannat*' If his words were for real, then I am going there in no time.

Because today, more than a decade later, I am in the same town. But this time around, I am not on a vacation. I am locked in a dark dungeon, with a sharp *khukri* in my neck. My throat slashed, blood dripping, my legs flicking, going berserk. Up-down, up-down. Right-left, left-right. Throwing themselves everywhere. Eyes popping out. My state is exactly like a freshly slaughtered goat on a Bakri-Eid morning.

I am dying. Very slowly, at a snail's pace, like the fat mouse that was guzzled by the python that summer evening at the Corbett park.

And I am extremely worried. Worried for *Zain* who had asked me to accompany him to the mosque and help him flick an umbrella. It was raining and Zain's parents were not buying him an umbrella. So he decided to steal one. We went inside the mosque with our skull caps on, and when the namaz started, we quietly sneaked out with one of the many umbrellas lying in a bucket outside. We had run with excitement and fear, our hearts pounding and thumping. And when we had run enough, we had called ourselves, 'The Umbrella Flickers.'

I am not worried about myself or my slashed throat. That worry is last on the list. Primarily I am concerned about my ammi, who is old now. The last time we met, she was no more the same. Not like the ammi of my childhood. She now walks with a stoop, her hair all white. I had asked her, 'why don't you apply henna to your hair ammi?'

Love, Lust & Lies

"Where is that kind of strength left in my bones? Let your wife come, I will make her apply some every weekend." I would blush, she would grin, and I would notice that a few of her teeth are also gone.

Worried about my abba, who is no more mobile. He lay down on his bed, looking at the ceiling all day long. Last time when I was home, he peed and shat on his bed. That was very disturbing.

And worried about *Zareen*, my only friend, my oldest friend.

And worried about *Priyanka*. The college bombshell. Will she be able to hold herself together after she comes to know of my demise?

But still, not too worried, because one of my friends, who helped me survive a monster called "*Bombay*" is already up there in heaven. I am pretty sure *Haider* has already booked the best bed for me in the heaven's dormitory. For he knows I am coming. Haider, my friend, can you just wait for a while. I have some last minute work pending.

I can clearly make out that my end is near. I saw this in some melodramatic Hindi movie, wherein the hero is dying and he could see flashbacks from his own life. I don't know how they knew this, but I am experiencing the same right now.

Probably, god gives you a chance to analyze your own life in the fading minutes in order to let you figure out your blunders and gaffes. Well, before we get into the details, let me tell you, I made a lot of them. Blunders and gaffes. And with them, I spoke *many ugly lies*. I never dared to share it all with anyone. But now, when my life is on the verge of getting over, I think I am brave enough to narrate a 'tell all tale.'

Pages from the book of my life are flipping rapidly. I can see all of them. Each episode, one by one. It's a bit hazy, but good enough. It's all coming back in the penultimate stage of my life. I am waiting for death to take over completely. But I know it will not, till the time I don't finish with my flashback, it won't.

Lets roll!

2nd

Abba was sitting on his favorite chair. Face blank, body still. Looking through the open window at the old Neem tree which was planted by my great-great-great grandfather. Obviously, he told me this. Several times. Beads in his hands, lips silently moving, muttering his prayers. He was seeking for some kind of a refuge in the old tree and the beads from the verbal abuse being hurled at him.

Apparently, I was big enough to be sent to some institute for my education, and ammi was not very gung-ho about the idea of me joining a madrasa. But Abba didn't cave in.

'What will he learn at a madrasa. Will become a recluse like you at the most?'

Abba dropped a bead.

'Look at Rahim *chacha's* son. He went to a school and is now working for some company in *Am-ree-kaaah*. Don't you want our son to earn like that?'

Abba dropped another bead.

'Ameen, come here.' She shouted, I rushed.

'Look, you know what, your abba doesn't want you to prosper. He doesn't give a hoot. He wants you to sit like him all your life in this rickety arm chair, with some beads in your hands.' She clinched her loose skin at the throat in-between her index finger and the thumb and announced, 'I *swear*, till I am alive, I am not going to allow this to happen. My son will not go to some madrasa and end a *jihadi* or a loner like you. He will....'
Abba's expression changed at this. The blank look was gone. The beads no more rolling. His face stiff, lines on his forehead shaky.

Very slowly he said, 'Am I a jihadi? Was my abba a jihadi? Do they really make jihadis at a madrasa? Do I want to stunt my own child's growth?' Nobody spoke for a second. 'The answer to all this is *no!* Yes, I am a loner, but I *choose* to be one. He can be whatever he wants to be. But he is not going to any school-*wool*. All my family members have been to a madrasa and he will also do the same. And that's final and binding.' Ammi made a few more hush-hush remarks, sobbed, and left the room. Abba as usual, back to his beads and the tree.

That was one of the few times I had seen abba retaliating. I was amazed and amused at the same time. This incidence made me realize that he was *actually* the patriarch of the family.

I was sitting in a corner, a little confused, a little scared, a mute spectator to all the drama that just unfolded. I didn't know what was the difference between a school and a madrasa. Even if I knew, they wouldn't have cared for my opinion anyway.

All my life I faced this ugly problem. Whenever I was nervous, things inside my stomach start moving. When they were fighting, it did move, but settled down a little later when abba called me in his typical style. Clucking his tongue, clicking his fingers, and chanting like a hyena, 'Ameen, *beta* come here.' In the first call, I would look at him, and in the second I would sprint and sit in his lap. That was the first time he showed me his 'Golden Diary.'

'Ameen, look at this. This is my *'sunahri kitaab.'* Golden Diary!' His eyes big enough to hold me. I had an open mouth when I got the first glimpse. The cover of the diary was golden and thus the name. It somewhat had a shimmering effect which would intrigue me much later as well. He opened it and flipped its pages several times to amuse me. Without a doubt, I was.

'Three things tell a man. His eyes, his friends, and his favorite *quotes,*' he said. I noticed there were things written in Urdu. 'You know what is written in here?' I shook my head. 'These are lines and quotations from the most famous, successful, intelligent, sought-after people who walked this planet. Albert Einstein, Gandhi, Nehru, Mother Teresa, Socrates, Oscar Wilde and many more.' Off course I didn't know any name of the lot, and was simply swinging my neck.

'I copied them all my childhood from a weekly Urdu magazine *'Buland-Awaaz.'* These thoughts helped me to be a better person and to lead a better life. They can guide you if you seriously dwell upon them. I will gift you this when you will mature enough to understand them.'

Out of the blue I asked a question which took abba by the neck.

'Abba, did they all go to a *madrasa*?' I still don't know if I was intelligent enough to think of such a question or if it was just a curious, regular child like question. But abba was not intelligent enough to find a suitable answer. He didn't reply. Closed his diary, lifted me up, kept me on the ground, gave a half smile, and left. I could see ammi sneaking from the door left ajar.

Generally, there used to be silence in the house for several days after ammi-abba had had a debate. The only noise used to be of footsteps, utensils being dropped in the kitchen, doors banging, and may be of the toilet flush. But surprisingly, this time they found an amiable solution quick.

My question probably had some affect on abba. At night they talked over this and thankfully better sense prevailed. I was not going to a madrasa where abba and his forefathers studied, but to a new, recently opened English medium madrasa. The idea of an English medium madrasa sounded novel and many parents, especially like my ammi, were sending their kids to learn this new art. Trust me, speaking English is no less than an art.

It made one thing very clear. Ammi didn't have a problem with a madrasa, but she desperately wanted me to learn English. According to her, it was going to be this language which will get me a job and help me more than any other thing I ever learn. She would instruct sternly at times, 'Learn *alif, bey, tey, sey* if you want to. But make sure that you learn A, B, C, D.'

Within a few days I was admitted in *"Darut Taleem Was-Sanat."* Abba bought me a new pair of white kurta-pajama, a new skull cap, a new water bottle, a new slate, a new bag and a few books. Wow! He bought me so many things without cribbing even once. They both wanted to give me quality education. And definitely they did.

Every morning, hand in hand with my ammi who used to be fully wrapped in a burqa and me in a uniform, water bottle hanging around my neck, swinging, slapping my tummy would go to my madrasa. In the evenings ammi would be back to pick me up.

Every morning she would tell me three things indifferently: Pay attention in your *English* class; Sit next to *studious* boys; *Don't* share your tiffin with anybody.

In the evenings she would ask me three things indifferently; What did the teacher teach you in the *English* class; Did you sit with studious boys; Did you eat your tiffin or share it with your *poor* friends.

Calling madrasa kids 'poor' used to rub abba the wrong way. So she manipulated and modified it to 'underprivileged' and reframed the question; 'Did you eat your tiffin or share it with your *underprivileged* friends.'

The day used to begin with all the kids singing *naats* - songs praising almighty, together in the main hall of the mosque. After that, the same hall was divided into several sections. Big

Love, Lust & Lies

boys, not so big boys, small boys, very small boys and then very-very small boys. We all used to be in the same hall, but hypothetically in different rooms. There were straw mats laid on the floors. One side was for the boys and the other for the girls.

The first hour used to be of Urdu, followed by Arabic language, English language and after *Zohar-* afternoon prayers, we all used to read the holy Quran before heading for our homes. On Fridays, English classes were chucked out as it used to be a half day.

All the teachers dressed in Kurta-pajama, most of them chewed tobacco throughout, some carried a small bamboo cane to create terror in our little hearts, few of them came on time and a very few smiled. In fact, smiling was an annual thing. Let's say Urdu *maulvi saheb* smiled today, then *Insha-Allah* you will see him smiling again after a year's time.

Within a few days, everybody had friends, except me. Thanks to my recluse half, I inherited from abba. It took some time, but soon I had. Sheezan and Zain hold the honor of becoming my first friends at madrasa.

I used to sit alone in one corner until one fine day these two devils, came and sat next to me. I *needed* to talk, and they *wanted* to talk. I needed, because I didn't have any friends, and they wanted to, in order to form a group. A troika, which would together rule the class, terrify everybody, and as Zain stated, 'We will be the *baap-* rulers of our class.' I don't know what he exactly meant by that, but it sounded exciting. I agreed.

Right then and there with that approval I went against all my ammi's instructions.

Breaking of Rule #1 & 2-: Sheezan and Zain were anything and everything under the sun, but studious, especially Zain. As far as English was concerned, the word "English" probably sounded as the name of some edible stuff to their ears.

Breaking of Rule #3-: We shared our lunch every day. It was a rule. Zain used to get four breads less the butter, Sheezan's box used to have an apple and two bananas chopped into as many pieces as possible. I used to get two *aloo parathas*. I badly wanted to follow ammi's third instruction. It was painful to watch the two loafers devour my *parathas* in minutes and offer me their breads and apples. Nevertheless, I had friends.

It used to be four in the afternoon by the time I used to return. Abba would be sitting on the same arm chair with his beads. Ammi would give me a bath and then make me finish my homework. English homework was to be completed first. In fact that was the only subject she checked personally. The irony here was, she knew all the subjects except English, but would not check any other subject except English.

I was free to do anything after that. I used to rush out of my house and dash into our neighbor's house. Because that was the home of Zareen. My oldest friend and my only friend, till Zain and Sheezan came into picture. We were friends since I don't remember. I don't know how we met, or how we became friends. I always knew her. We would run to the tree behind her house, and would collect all the berries that squirrels would drop from their mouths, and then compete to finish them. We played with an old tyre of a truck that we discovered in the bushes. Rolling it with a bamboo stick and running behind it all around.

She was still not going to any madrasa or school. Neither were her parents interested. She would ask infinite curious questions on my madrasa. I would proudly tell her all.

'It's so much fun out there.'

'I have so many friends.'

'We share our lunch.'

'I am learning *English*.'

Love, Lust & Lies

'We play during lunch time, oh, I just don't want to return, but the bell rings. Blah blah blah.....'

I would boast endlessly. Only a few points used to be true though, rest all were plain and simple lies. I loved to watch that greed on her face. Greed to attend madrasa like me. Greed to make friends like me. Greed to share her lunch box like me. Greed to do everything I was doing.

One day she had asked 'Are there girls in your madrasa?'

'No! Girls don't come, it's only for boys.' I had lied again. I was scared that may be she will convince her parents to send her to a madrasa as well. She will be square with me. I wanted to boast all my life. I wanted to see that greedy expression on her face all my life. It made me feel superior and better in some eccentric way.

In the evenings when I would return, abba would be glued to the television screen watching news on Doordarshan. The only television channel that used to come then. Those days they were talking about a young boy with extremely curly hair, enormously talented and was looked upon as the next Gavaskar and the future of Indian cricket. He was just 21 and had already scored hell lot of centuries. This young boy's name was Sachin Tendulkar.

On some days the ghost of *Babri-Masjid* would return on news and haunt abba. The pictures of people climbing up the mosque and bringing it to ground with spears would disturb him. If there was news on Babri Masjid, he would retire to bed early, leaving me and ammi alone to watch the serials. On other days he would sit till late.

The favorite show of our family used to be *Alif Laila*. A series based on the stories from "The Arabian Nights." It began with Scheherazade telling stories to *Shahryar*. Stories of Sinbad the Sailor and his Seven Voyages, Ali Baba And The Forty Thieves, Aladdin And His Magical Lamp, The Merchant And The Genie, The

Fisherman And The Genie. All of it used to appeal and fascinate me big time. Though the biggest shows then were 'The Mahabharata' and 'Ramayana,' it was banned in our home for reasons that are better not explained. I guess you are intelligent enough to make that out.

The whole town that year went mad for Salman Khan and Madhuri Dixit when they came together in a movie called *"Hum Aapke Hain Kaun."* Almost everyone had already watched it, but the crowds were still flocking in. Men, ladies, children, everybody went crazy. It was being considered as the biggest hit. Even bigger than *"Sholay."*

We never went to the local cinema hall. There was a shop which used to give video cassettes on rent along with the VCR. Whenever there was a movie which the whole town was raving about, we used to get the two and the whole family would enjoy it together. Zareen also used to join us. She loved the *lehengas* and other beautiful dresses Madhuri flaunted. So did ammi. I liked Salman Khan and his macho style. I don't know what abba liked, but he watched the whole movie attentively.

After the movie, Zareen was asked by her ammi to get some groceries from the local market. She asked me to give her company. All our way she kept gibbering about the movie. So much was she smitten by it that she didn't care to ask me even one question on my madrasa. After buying the required stuff she requested to walk a few more steps to the local theater.

Soon we were standing outside the main gates of the theater watching the huge poster on display. Salman was holding Madhuri in a very sensuous pose. Giving a peck on her neck. Zareen was disappointed. It only had their faces. She wanted to see her *lehenga*. We stood there for a while, watching the mad crowd bustling in, buying tickets, children with their parents and all the energy around.

'I don't know if I will ever be able to go and watch a *filim* here. These kids are so lucky,' Zareen said with a gloomy face.

'I promise we will go to watch the next movie.' A smile graced her face, 'You promise, right.'

'Yeah, we will go for sure, but there must be Salman Khan in the movie.'

'No, we will go for a film starring Madhuri Dixit.'

' Salman!' 'Madhuri!' 'Salman!' 'Madhuri!'

We went back quarrelling. I had made her a promise which I had no idea how will I fulfill. But whenever she was around, my boastful part used to take over. And I would end up giving similar hollow promises. The need to show my weight used to get double when she was around.

Months flew by and I was pretty much comfortable in my madrasa. I was familiar with the roads as well. Though ammi still used to pick me up in the afternoon, in the mornings I went alone.

Some politician had come that day to our madrasa. We were made to sit in a line on the ground, opposite to the mosque, right under the burning sun. The *khadi* clad minister was sitting on a stage specially made for him and his brigade. Finally, after an hour or so, his highness came to the dais to speak 'two words.' But when these white collar thugs come on the stage, be sure that the two words will become two million or so. Every now and then a boy would faint due to the heat. A maulvi would rush, silently take him away in his arms, making sure that no one notices. The minister was wearing a Ray-Ban aviator and barking all what he has done for the Muslim community. In between someone would clap. He would take a sip of water and bark again. This process would repeat several times. Finally he made the announcement he had come to make.

'There are so many kids out here and I have good news for them. I am making a basket ball court right here, where you all are sitting. This is a new game, an American game, which you will enjoy a lot. I hope your teachers and parents like it and vote for me in the coming elections so that I can serve you all and make many more basketball courts. Thank you, Jai hind!'

The minister left with his brigade in a fleet of cars and we were more than happy to see him go. The heat was unbearable by now and we dashed back in our classes.

'What is a basket ball court?' I inquired.

'I don't know,' said Zain. Sheezan had some rough idea.

'There is a big ball, unlike cricket, but very much like a football. And there is a net hanging on a pole. You have to throw the ball in the net and score a goal.

'And whoever scores the maximum is the winner, right.' This was my contribution.

'Yeah, but the term is something different for a goal.........Aaahh, I think.......I think....I don't remember what exactly they call a goal in basketball. But yeah, it is played somewhat like that.' He tried hard to recall the term, but as usual, failed.

At home I told ammi-abba about the minister and his announcement. Ammi was delighted.

'Is it an American game?' Her eyes electrified, 'Ameen, you must learn that game.' The word America used to charge her up. Abba didn't pay much heed to the basketball part but the minister.

'These ministers will only come to our madrasa when the elections are approaching. They know that we are stupid enough to be fooled easily by a basketball court for votes.'

Ammi snapped, 'you are such a pessimist. Thank god we produced so many babies and have a huge voting population. At

Love, Lust & Lies

least these politicians find us important enough to make a *baaskit-bowl* for our kids.'

Now along with English I also had the responsibility of learning this silly game. I promised myself not to use the word "America" in front of ammi ever again. But to be honest, these two things helped me a lot later in life. You never know what comes handy when. Life is something where you need to expect the unexpected to happen.

As a quote in my abba's golden diary says-:
"Life is what happens to you when you are busy making other plans."
JOHN LENNON

So true. Isn't it?

It's been almost a year since the minister had come to the madrasa and made the announcement of making a basketball court. Though it should have been ready by now, it was comforting to see the construction work at least kicking off. It was expected to be complete *anytime*. Please make a note of the word 'anytime.' This word evokes positive hope and keeps everyone calm and patient.

On the other end, the troika of me, Zain and Sheezan was doing well together. We didn't become the *baap* of our class as Zain had promised, but Zain definitely became the *baap* of our troika. The fatso always had the last word. He has to be the most cunning, scheming, wily, sly and shrewd kid god ever made. I will tell you Why? Can one imagine a ten year old madrasa boy having a crush on a *hijab* wearing madrasa girl. No ways! This thought never crossed my mind and I can bet, it didn't cross any other boy's mind as well. In-fact, I never noticed that there are girls in our class, and that of a different sex actually. But Zain did.

I remember the bell for the lunch break had just struck and all the kids rushed out of their classes. If a *firangi*-white man, ever saw that scene, kids in kurta-pajamas with skull caps on their heads, running out from all corners, shouting like hooligans, I can bet he will run away in fear taking it for a terror camp where young Muslim kids are being taught jihad.

Zain was not in a mood to play or eat that particular lunch break. He was a little lost. To see him quiet was actually more unnerving.

'Guys, I like Rubina?' Thankfully he spoke, but what in the hell was that?

'Who is Rubina?' I and Sheezan asked in unison.

'*She* sits opposite to me.' Both amazed at the use of pronoun 'she.'

'Any ideas how I can be friends with her?' Both mute now.

'You two morons can never come up with any productive ideas. I will have to think on my own.' Both abashed but glad we don't need to think.

'We will throw paper balls to catch her attention.' Both petrified now. Both terrified now. Both regretting for not thinking of some sane ideas.

'Zain *bhai*, we will be rusticated if maulvi catches us doing that. Didn't you see what maulvi did to Qasim when he forgot to get his slate. He placed a pencil in-between his fingers and pressed it hard mercilessly. Qasim cried so much. God knows what maulvi may do if he catches us doing such a disgraceful thing. We are not even allowed to talk to them and...'

Sheezan was cut short by Zain, 'screw the Maulvis. Are girls Martians or Satans that we can't talk to them. Are you both impotents? Will you guys throw paper balls or no?' Both too scared to agree and too ashamed to back-off. Courtesy, the use of word "impotent."

'Who else can I look for support apart from you both? You guys are my only friends. I promise that this will be the last favor I am asking for. I just want one chance to introduce myself and then I alone will take it forward from there.'

He had played his trump card well. Get the emotional aspect into picture, it will always work. India is a country of emotional fools. I swear, that particular minute he looked like a distant cousin of that minister. We agreed. But was there an option? One needed balls to say 'No' to Zain. Unfortunately, we didn't have then. It was decided to execute the plan the following day just after the Arabic class gets over and English class is about to commence.

That evening, while returning, I again pleaded with ammi not to come in the evenings to pick me up.

'I am big enough to come back. Why do you take the trouble? I know the roads.' I said, handing over my bag and water bottle.

Ammi retorted, 'I know that you are big enough. But why should I rob myself of an opportunity of coming out from that shanty of your abba's. It's kind of a small vacation for me. It gives me a taste of freedom.'

'Freedom! Huh! You look so trapped under that veil. You look like a haunted black figure. Why don't you take it off?' She didn't speak. With some effort I could see her eyes under the translucent cloth. She was contemplating, a little apprehensive of the consequences. When all of a sudden she flipped the cloth covering her face. She was smiling, genuinely looking happy. Free in the true sense of the word. Like a bird that has just been rescued from a cage, goes high up in the sky and swirls several times. Ammi was looking around with wide open eyes.

Ammi's freedom was short lived. She covered her face back. Later she quipped, 'that was an experience of a life time.' It sounded as if she had been on some adventure trip. She added, 'life is not about the number of breaths you take, but the number of moments that take your breath away. Unfortunately in my life there have been very few.' There was a slight husk in her voice when she spoke that last line.

That was the first and the only time I ever saw her face outside my own house. Oh god, she looked beautiful.

Just before entering our house ammi warned me not to mention a word about her little adventure in front of abba. I nodded. Abba was watching the evening news. They were talking about a pneumonic plague epidemic in Gujarat that had resulted in many deaths and a large internal migration of about three hundred thousand residents, who fled fearing quarantine. A combination of heavy monsoon rain and clogged sewers led to massive flooding which resulted in unhygienic conditions and a number of unclean animal carcasses. The lady on television with a huge round, dark maroon *"bindi"* stamped on her forehead, speaking like a robot added, 'there was widespread fear that the flood of refugees might spread the epidemic to other parts of India and the world, but that scenario was averted, probably because of effective public health response mounted by the Indian health authorities.'

"Can you believe that? They are giving credit to *Indian health authorities*. As if they exist. Huh!" Abba sarcastically said.

Bakri-Eid was approaching and I overheard abba telling ammi about getting three instead of two goats this year. One each to be sacrificed in the name of ammi-abba and one for *me*. Exclusively for me. Wow, I exclaimed for two reasons; I was important enough for a goat to be sacrificed in my name, and there will be goats in the house and I and Zareen could play with them for hours.

Next day at madrasa the Arabic class was coming to an end. One could easily see beads of sweat on my and Sheezan's forehead. Zain was cool and composed as always, his hands busy mashing and rolling paper sheets, with a grin on his face. He passed us a paper ball each.

'The moment maulvi *sahib* leaves, throw this on the girl sitting third from left.' Zain hissed in our ears pointing with his index finger.

'Zain, are you sure we need to do this?' Sheezan made a last attempt to change his mind.

'Don't talk like a bozo. Don't throw if you don't want to But never show us your face again. Ameen tell him that.'

'Yeah... just throw it on her. It will be over in a split second.' To be honest, I wanted to agree with Sheezan, but Zain's scare was fiercer than any maulvi's.

The bell rang, and with it our hearts started thumping. Sheezan was sweating like a pig. We picked our weapons, waiting for our general's command.

'NOW!'

Three paper missiles went flying towards Rubina. Mine was not on target, Sheezan could not gather enough strength and his missile landed half way. Zain struck bull's eye.

'Who threw that?' Exclaimed Rubina. The little small balls of mine froze. And I can say that on Sheezan's behalf as well. We remained terrified until Zain spoke.

'Oh, that is my paper roll. It was a mistake. Can you please return that.' I liked the way he changed paper ball into a paper roll.

'What kind of a mistake is this?' She threw the ball back. It covered more distance than Sheezan's throw.

'I am sorry for that. Thank you....aunh.... What is your good name?' Zain asked. I couldn't believe my ears. He used the words *sorry* and *thank-you* in one sentence.

'Rubina!'

'Zain here.'

The ice was broken and Zain if not much, was very happy. Unbelievable! That was the first time I witnessed the effect of a girl on a boy's conduct. Everything takes a 360 degree turn.

'See, that was so easy.' Zain winked at us. We both had declared, *"wah, bandey mein aukaat hai."*- this boy got guts. We were proud of our boss. He really made it look so easy.

That evening abba told me to come with him to the local market. We were going to buy goats for bakri-eid. Unlike ammi, he was not holding my hand. That was good in a way. I felt important and thought that I have matured. After all, I am big enough for a goat to be sacrificed in my name. I tried imitating abba. Walking slowly with a slight stoop. My back soon ached and I stood straight again.

A few urchins were playing nearby. All naked, grubby, careless and reckless.

'They all are as thin as my little finger. Doctors would never need their X-rays. This is just a small sample of all the *Muslim* kids in our country suffering from this heinous disease. All are malnourished.' I don't know how he knew their religion and I didn't care about the disease.

'Do you know what it is to be malnourished?' Abba asked. I shook my head.

'When you have a face of a boy and a belly of a buffalo, or alternatively, your face looks like a football, your bones can be counted with naked eye and your body is standing on two stumps of cricket, that is when you are malnourished.' I used my creative head to imagine what it is to be one. 'Quite ugly,' I thought.

'Every second a child dies due to this noxious disease. But all these ministers care for is a *basketball* court.'
By the time abba stopped spitting venom we had reached the market. The atmosphere smelled of goats and their excreta. There were chubby goats and slender goats. There were goats with two horns, one horn and a few were hornless. All bleating as if they know their end is near.

'To select the right goat is also an art. You have to select the most beautiful goat.' Now that really puzzled me. They all look the same. How can one say that the goat sleeping in that corner is more or less beautiful than the one shitting out here, I thought.

'Check if their teeth are proper, if the shape of their horns is nice, the goat must be as fat as possible and must be healthy.'

We looked for the goat with all the mentioned qualities, but were unable to get one for quite a time. The problem was not with the goats, but was with my abba's wallet. The rates of the so called beautiful goats were very high. In fact, that was the most important factor in front of which all the other factors looked meek. My abba's wallet was not fat enough to fetch a fat goat.

After a lot of loitering, checking the goats by putting fingers in their nostrils, and in-between their teeth, he settled for two black and a white goat. The white one was of supreme quality with all the teeth in place and all the horns intact. While the two blacks were of second grade. I held the white one while abba gave company to the remaining two. Right from the second I came to know that the white one is costlier, I had set my priorities straight.

We reached home and the goats were given a corner under the backyard porch. Zareen came in and I told her flat, 'the *white* one is mine.' Zareen analyzed the black goats for a good two minutes before selecting the smaller one. I was happy I had a bigger goat.

I named my goat 'Prem,' the name of Salman Khan's character in *Hum Aapke Hain Kaun*. Zareen followed and named her goat Nisha, the name of Madhuri Dixit's character. Now this irritated me big time.

'You can't do that. This goat is a male. It's insulting to call him by a female name. The goat will feel humiliated. Come on, change the name.'

'Oh Ameen, how does it matter. I like the name Nisha. It's my goat, let me call it by a name I want to.'

'You are just a copycat. Use your creative head for a different name.' I snapped.

'I don't know how to be creative. I don't go to a madrasa like you. I don't get to read books. I am not educated enough.' I swear I wanted to hear that. I allowed her.

For the next few days we played with our goats as much as we could. Gave them a wash, taught them tricks, fed them. Obviously the freshest and the juiciest of the grass would go to Prem and leftovers were for the other two. Zareen was not always around and I didn't care for her goat.

Finally it was Bakri-Eid, and time to say goodbye to our friends. Abba selected Prem to go first. With a heavy heart I brought him forward. Gave him a wash for one last time. The butcher in a flash turned him upside down. Prem was bleating, I could see my picture in his eyeballs. As if pleading to save him. I was helpless. He was irrepressible. Abba told me to hold Prem's leg. I held them tight. Patted his tummy. He went quiet. The Maulvi moved his lips, said the prayers and slowly tore open his throat. Blood came out like water from a fountain. My Kurta had a few blood stains and my eyes had a few tears. Prem was no more.

Nisha was next. I went ahead to hold his legs as well. He was repulsive. I tried and tried, but failed. He didn't let me touch him. As if telling me to keep my dirty hands off him. For all the partiality, for all the green grass I robbed him off. I made one last try, and he kicked me in my stomach hard. My bones started shivering. heart thumping. I backed off, thanking my stars that my crotch was still in shape. Abba stepped in to hold the goat. Nisha became a lot more calmer.

Zareen was watching all this from a distance. Is she thinking the same, I thought. Of course she was. The disgusting look on her face was more than a proof of that.

Seasons changed and winter chills gripped our town. Winters are much more quite. Peaceful. The *ZZZZ* sound of fans and coolers are no more heard. It's you and your blankets. In the mornings while going to madrasa I used to wear a monkey cap. Thick layers of fog would make things more difficult. Sometimes so thick that one couldn't see his own nails. You simply walk hoping that the manhole is not open. The breeze used to be so cold and sharp that it could cut one's face open cold-bloodedly.

The good news was, at madrasa the basket ball court was done. Big boys were playing that lunch break with a big orange ball. Nobody knew the rules, but who cares. Get hold of the ball, run and throw it in the net. Basketball had arrived. I and Zain tried it later. Sheezan was not there because he was no more a part of our troika. Zain chucked him out of our group.

Apparently, whenever Sheezan used to get something delicious, rather than his chopped bananas in his tiffin, he would eat a portion discreetly before the lunch break, and then join us with the remaining. I used to feel that his ammi is selfish and a hungry creature who chucks half his lunch in the morning. Until Zain, 'the hawk eyed' caught him. Sheezan was mortified, Zain repulsive. Result, we two decided to boycott him. It was more 'he' who decided, than 'we' actually.

"All these studious nerds are the same. Hypocrites and backstabbers," Zain fumed. Sheezan no more used to sit or hang around with us. I would talk to him sometimes. He didn't have new friends yet. But looked happier. His eyes would taunt, *'at least I am not a slave of that obese animal anymore.'* He was free and that is probably what mattered to him the most.

That night I couldn't sleep. May be because Sheezan was free and I was not. I didn't let my ammi sleep either and asked her to tell me a story. It was something like this-:

Once a sailor caught a crow who could speak. The sailor was elated. He would be rich by organizing shows of the speaking crow, he thought. But much to his disappointment the crow never spoke after getting caught. He always kept silent. The sailor tried to woo him by providing him with the best of amenities. But nothing worked.

Soon the sailor was going on a trip across the sea once again. He was just about to leave when the crow spoke; 'Can you go to the kingdom beyond the blue mountains where my family lives. I will always be grateful to you if you can inform my grandfather that I am fine and in the best of health. If you do so, I promise I will continue speaking the same way.' The sailor agreed. As promised, he visited the crow's family. He met his grandfather and informed him, 'Your grandson is with me. He is fine and in the best of health.'

Hearing this, the old crow suddenly fell and died. The sailor felt sad, but he could not do much. He left. When he returned, he narrated the incidence. The crow when came to know of his grandfather's demise, he fell and died as well. The sailor felt guilty of killing not one but two birds. He decided to give him a proper burial at least. He dug a small place in his backyard where the crow could be laid down to rest. Then he brought the crow's body outside. The moment he kept his body on the ground, the crow flew. The sailor was astonished.

Before leaving, the crow gibed, 'My grandfather taught me this trick. He told me, everyone has a right to be free. A little lie doesn't matter if it gets you some.' And the crow flew away free of all the hassles.

After hearing that story I always tried to create a lie, a plan, a tactic by which I could get my ammi the freedom she deserves. Free of her veil, free to live her life as she always longed for, free like the birds, the clouds, and the breeze. Regrettably, I am looking for the tactic till now.

"Freedom always looks small when you have it in your hands, but let it go and you would realize, how big and precious it is."

After all everyone deserves to be free!

4th

Zain had carried it forward very well with Rubina. He used to transform into somebody totally unlike him, a thorough gentleman, when the girl was around. There were innumerous changes in him. His kurtas were stainless now, hair oiled and combed, was using cologne to smell nice, making sure that he picks his nose at the right moment, and above all, he was refraining from using any kind of profanity. Suddenly madrasa was abuzz with rumors that Zain has been to the local theater with Rubina to catch the latest offering. A new movie which was winning hearts all around. This movie's name was *'Dilwale Dulhaniya Le Jayenge.'*

But nobody was really sure if Zain had actually been there, and that too with Rubina. I dared to clear the air straight from the horse's mouth. We both were sitting on one of the many benches, watching some boys play basketball.

'Zain, have you seen the latest movie they are talking about?' I asked. He nodded.

I went a step forward, 'Did you go with Rubina?' There was no response this time and I didn't ask again. A little later he spoke, 'How do you know that?'

'Everybody knows that. I was not sure so I asked you.' We went quiet again.

That evening Zareen had the same movie on mind. She reminded me of my promise. I tried ignoring her but she would get back. I tried to bury the topic by reminding her of the sacrosanct requisite.

'There is no Salman Khan or even your Madhuri Dixit in that movie.'

'But everybody is going crazy behind that movie. Let's go, please.'

'You don't get it Zareen. And above that, where will we get the money from, and what if we get caught? I will get the video cassette if you want to watch it so desperately.'

'It's not just about watching the movie Ameen. It's about watching one in a *theater*.' She was quite for a second before she sulked again, 'I will never be able to watch a movie in there. You are my last hope Ameen.' She said with a dismal face. Though I always loved to see that expression on her face, I didn't like it this time.

'Alright, I will try.' I told her for the time being. I thought, may be Zain can help me with some of his smart tips.

The same night there was a marriage in town. Some Salim and Rukhsana were getting solemnized for life. One of the most incredible things about a wedding ceremony in a small town is, that almost the whole town is invited. No matter if you are related or not, or even if you don't know who is getting married. *You* are invited. The little few who are not invited are also welcome. Even the dogs of the town know where they will get their dinner for the night. So all the people and all the dogs head for the venue to hog in as much as possible.

One more peculiar thing about Muslim marriages is that men and women don't sit together. The whole venue is divided into two sections with the help of a cotton cloth. The cloth acts as the boundary or the border which defines the parameters within which ladies and gents can roam around. But the irony is, nobody cares a fuck. Most of the men, especially the 18-23 year olds, who are touted to be the next grooms, visit the ladies section to show off their colorful *sherwanis* and their ugly oily hairstyles. The ladies are no less with their extremely bright red lipsticks and loud make-ups. Actually the whole ladies-gents concept is to give the

'Muslim marriage feel.' If you don't adhere to this, some maulvi may issue a *fatwa*. The bottom-line is, it's all hypocrisy.

There is also a very interesting set of people at these functions. This set just concentrates on the food. The moment the counters start serving, they rush and gobble as much as they can. These people then go for a long-nice walk. Soon they are back in the queue, ready to gobble a fresh plate again. Their mantra is simple, gobble-walk-gobble.

Zain was also there in a black kurta pajama, looking suave and more. He visited the ladies section with an excuse of seeing his ammi several times. *"Yeah right! As if I don't know. Suddenly so much love for your ammi, Zain,"* I thought.

After a while when Zain was done with his visits, we took a plate each and sat down with our chicken tikkas and rumali rotis. Zain only had leg pieces in his plate. I counted, 'one, two, three, four, five. Five of them. *Oh no!* There was one more secretly lying behind the salad. Six of them. Phew!' The fatso really ate like a fatso. He would eat the meat and feed the bone to the dog sitting next to him. The dog would finish it in seconds, and again drop his tongue with saliva leaking like a tap left lose. After a couple of more helpings, Zain was done and I was dying to ask him the question.

'How did you manage to take Rubina to the local theater?'

'Why? Are you also planning to take somebody?' I don't know how his sly mind made that out. But I knew that if I ever wanted him to tell me that, I had to give him a lucrative excuse.

'Yeah! There is somebody.' And then he laughed his head off.

He! He! He! He! He! There was no end to his hysterics. I could see particles of meat still stuck between his molars and canines clearly. Zain holding his tummy, with tears in his eyes, asked, 'who is the ill-omened girl?'

I had to tell him everything before he opened his gutter of a mouth and give me the idea. But only after asking a few more absurd questions that were still bouncing in his mind, 'Do you like her?'

'No, absolutely no. it's just that she is a friend, and man, she sulks. I can't bear her sulking in front of me.' I was sure of every word I had said, till Zain spoke next.

'Dude, you don't like her. Why the pains then?' I gave him an ignorant look. He continued, 'Anyways, the best time is the morning show. 11 to 2.'

'But that's during madrasa. How is that possible?'

'That's the key. Nobody will ever think you are anywhere else but madrasa. Tell her to give some excuse at her place and you bunk that day.' Zain was sounding insane, but there was some smartness in his insanity. He continued, 'the tickets are twenty-five rupees each. Let the man charge the normal rates. Don't tell him that you are a minor or he may ask for your parents and you will be screwed right then and there. It's kind of a bribe to shut him up.'

'What about the attendance?'

'You kidding me. There is no such thing called attendance in our madrasa. But if you are so worried, I will shout on your behalf.' I could trust Zain on that. He used to find some kind of a solace in doing such outrageous activities. Answering the roll call in class on other's behalf was one of his favorite pastimes.

Soon the bride was shedding a drain full of tears and her parents and another millions of relatives sat there grabbing them. Finally the groom's father had to intervene to cut short the melodrama and the bride left in a brand new red Maruti 800.

Love, Lust & Lies

Within minutes, people walked out of the place leaving the dogs and bones lying around.

On our way back, ammi, abba were discussing the food, bride's dress, groom's family and the red Maruti. Abba liked all, except the red Maruti, 'I don't know why these fools ask for dowry. These mullahs will issue a *fatwa* for every other thing but won't interfere in matters which are of prime importance.' Abba's face turned as red as the car.

'But why are you getting worried? Let people who have daughters fret over this. Why should we care?' Ammi had a lot of hopes from my marriage I suppose. I remember her saying at times, 'it's your destiny to get a poor father, but you are the only one who can be blamed for a poor father-in-law.'

But there was a bigger brawl waiting to happen. Ammi was apparently not happy with my progress in English. It was more than two years now in madrasa and I could not construct a single sentence. Agreed that the time is less, but ammi expected me to learn it in a jiffy. Every passing day would make her swell with anger, anxiousness and grief. It would all come out on abba.

'See what your madrasa has done to our son's future. It's ruined. It's over even before it started. He doesn't know even a bit of English. I blew my lid off shouting, pleading, begging you to send him to a school, but no, because your family members, who all are rubes, went to a madrasa, you won't bow down.' Abba would calmly reply, 'Najma, be a little patient. It's just a matter of time before he picks it up.' Ammi would go quiet for a few days before returning with more virulence.

But all I was bothered these days was to chalk out a plan to take Zareen for the movie. The next evening I told her about my not so confident plan.

'We need three things for the movie. One, fifty rupees. Two, a lot of guts, and three, ability to tell a white lie.' I was very confident with my lies, but Zareen had to lie in this case, and I was apprehensive about that.

'I will tell ammi that I am going to see a friend who is ill.' Zareen said when I asked if she had any excuses at hand.

'And money.'

'Don't worry, I will get that.' Zareen said with a flat face. I didn't ask much, as I was glad that she had made all the arrangements. We decided for the next day.

I was unable to sleep that night. I remember this very clearly. Kept on changing sides, thinking if I should drop the plan. But the thought that Zareen will consider me a coward used to keep me in. Will I be able to boast with same panache, with the same vigor and confidence. *No!* My ticket for self assertion will be lost.

As planned, I didn't go to madrasa, but to the market. There was a deserted narrow street, just a couple of steps from the local theater. I had to sit and wait there for more than two hours till Zareen arrived. Trust me, the long wait was like watching a movie in itself. Sitting idle with hundreds of ugly thoughts crossing your mind can be tormenting.

That dingy lane was home to many creatures. A couple of dogs were sleeping nearby. Behind me, up on the walls there were many lizards relaxing. On the ground there were millions of ants moving in a linear fashion. An extremely fat mouse came out from a small opening, realized that there is an unfamiliar visitor, hence he whooshed back in. I was sure he will attack me soon with his friends. I was getting more and more nervous. I didn't visit the toilet that morning and that was making things worse. That thing inside my stomach could have popped out causing much embarrassment, but thankfully Zareen showed up. I had never been so delighted to meet anyone before.

We still had half an hour in our hands. Generally the morning shows are not full, so we got the tickets easily. As Zain had instructed, I didn't ask for any discounts or for anything else, but the tickets. Zareen was covered head to toe, except the face. She was extremely excited. No signs of nervousness at all.

Soon the gates were opened. People started flocking in. We joined the queue. The man at the gate took our tickets, tore it and gave us a half with a suspicious look on his face. In fact, everybody in there was glaring at us.

I hate it! I hate it! I hate it. This is the thing I have always hated about small towns. Everybody knows everybody's business. I mean it's nice sometimes as they're always there to help you out. But at times they're like waiting for something awful to happen to help you out. And when nothing awful happens, they just sit around and talk about what's happening which is none of their business. I was hoping that nobody catches us there, or the news will spread like fire.

With every step, we both were discovering things which were knocking us for a six.

'Ya Allah, it's so dark out here. It's such a huge hall, such a huge screen and thousands of chairs. Why are people whistling? Why is the volume so high? Why this interval? Why the toilets are so dirty?' Questions, questions and more questions sprung one after the other and the movie ended.

The hero was not very good looking, but a charmer. I realized that girls may resist the looks, but can't resist the charm. For he in the end took the heroine with him in a train. I walked out of the theater with Zareen. Our heads were spinning. The movie was fine but it left us with a kind of hangover. Zareen found the actor quite handsome, especially his two deep dimples. I thought he was wearing a wig.

Zareen rushed back to her house and I to my madrasa, hoping ammi hasn't arrived yet to pick me up. She had not. I waited outside till she came and we both walked back. I was glad that everything went according to the plan, but as they say, 'it's not over till it's over.'

There were sounds of a woman yelling from the next door. Apparently, Zareen's ammi had found out that she was not at any of her friend's place and was livid.

'Where were you, tell me honestly Zareen, or else I swear I will thrash you dead.' Zareen's sob could be heard clearly. My heart started pounding.

'Moo...movie...' Zareen fumbled.

'What? You went to watch a movie. *filim!* With whom?' She didn't speak, kept silent. The thing in my stomach which had by now settled down, made movements again. I was praying nonstop. *Zareen, please don't take my name, please, I beg you. I swear, I will be ever grateful to you. I will.....*

And guess what? Zareen didn't.

'I went alone. I took out money from abba's wallet. I went alone, all alone,' she yelled back.

One doesn't need to think hard to make out what followed next. She was thrashed, abused, and locked in some corner of her house. And all this while, I stood in my own house like a coward, like a chicken, a quitter, a weakling, a deserter, a runaway. I don't have enough words to abuse myself. I didn't gather enough courage to go up and save my best friend, my only friend. At times Zain would ask, 'Ameen, are you a *fattu* - a scared cat or something?'

I had my answer that evening, *Yes I am.*

Those days cricket world cup was on. And as any other Indian, abba was following it religiously. India was in the Semi-Finals. We were playing Sri Lanka at the Eden Gardens, chasing 252 and were going fine when lightning struck. We slumped from 98/1 to 120/8. Eden Garden started burning. People in the stadium created havoc. Match was declared over and Sri Lanka was declared as the winner. Vinod Kambli left the field in tears. India was no more in the run for the coveted cup. The only good thing was that Sachin Tendulkar, the young boy they had talked about on news years before, was the highest scorer that series.

Abba became a huge fan of this little man. So much so that he bought a cricket bat for me. Though I had a cricket bat now, but Basketball till then had taken priority. I picked up the game quick. I told ammi about my developments. She was happy with that part but as usual worried about my English.

One day after madrasa, I saw her standing with another *burqa* clad woman. Two black haunted figures in a conversation, something terrible will follow soon, was my guess. I didn't know what they talked about till we reached home.

'You know *what* somebody told me today. The English teachers at Ameen's madrasa are *worse* than the teachers at a *government* school. Did you hear that, *worse* than government school teachers.' Ammi was at it again.

Now even comparing somebody with a government teacher is a huge insult. Here she stated that they were worse than them. The lady outside the madrasa had selected the right words.

'How will he learn English when the teacher himself doesn't know any. These days, knowing English is vital. A person who doesn't know English has no self esteem, ego or respect. Please send him to a school.'

Abba replied in his ever creative style, 'every time I walk out of my house and bump into somebody, do you know what they say. They say salaam Jalal *sahib*. *Jalal sahib*. That *sahib* is a mark of respect you were talking about, and I have all that without knowing an iota of English.' Abba always had some or the other riposte ready. He used to speak less, but was bang on target always.

It was almost a year since I and Zareen went to the local theater. She was no more allowed out of her house alone, and I didn't have nerves to visit her. Not seeing Zareen for so long was very difficult. I wanted to tell her lot of things. Share my opinion whether I should be sent to a school, debate if Sachin Tendulkar is the greatest batsmen as abba says, question why our favorite serial Alif Laila has gone off air, basketball, Zain, Sheezan, about every other thing under the sun. I was missing Zareen.

All this while a lot happened according to the news channels around India. Dr. I. K. Gujaral was replaced by Mr. Atal Behari Vajpayee as the prime minister of the country. India celebrated its 50th year of independence. Cricketer Raman Lamba died on the field. Lalu Prasad Yadav was stuck in a fodder scam, and down south Jayalalitha in TANSI land case. Match fixing came into picture. Sourav Ganguly and Rahul Dravid were new cricket sensations. Onion politics scandal. A. R. Rehman released his version of Vandey Mataram. Chandra-Kanta became the biggest serial on television. Chaiya-Chaiya was biggest song. A sheep was cloned, the great Mother Teresa was no more.

So much happened around but our town remained unaffected. Forget the town, nothing changed in our small two rooms, a hall and a toilet home. I sometimes used to wonder if my town actually falls in India. Ammi kept on taunting and harassing abba to send me to a school. Abba ignored. She would promise that we both will not be able to see her face again as she will run away. But she will be right in front of us the next morning. She would promise she will commit suicide, but will be very much alive the next morning.

And then she fell ill one day. I would say she was kind of lucky to fall ill at the right moment. There was still enough time for the schools to take new admissions and my madrasa year to end.

Lying on her bed, with miserable and helpless eyes she still fought for my right. We all thought she will be no more. Her time has come. And she took advantage of this fact to the hilt. Ammi would open her eyes, ask abba if he is ready to send me to a school, wait for a reply, and close her eyes. Again open, wait, close, open-wait-close, open-wait-close. Finally abba said the big "YES," she was waiting for.

Here abba promised to send me to a school, and there ammi regained her health. Abba was always besides her. It was then that I noticed abba's love for ammi. He was not romantic or charming like Shah Rukh Khan, but his love for ammi was unconventional. I learnt that you don't need to be macho or super cool to love somebody.

So, after being a rebel for more than two years, ammi had her way. After all, nobody achieved anything without a bit tussle and scuffle. She finally was going to realize her dream of seeing me off to a school. She was so happy that when she fully recovered, she cooked *haleem*, a dish she last cooked on her first day in the kitchen after marriage, and then it was now.

Last few days at madrasa were just as usual. Zain was happy with Rubina and used to wink sometimes during the class to showoff, Sheezan was happy with his freedom and with his tiffin, and I was just living life as it comes.

I was a little apprehensive of going to a completely new and a strange place. I shared my nervousness with abba. He simply quoted a line from his diary-:

A ship is safest at the shore. But that is not what it is built for.

'You are the first from our family who will be going to a school. You are built for more Ameen.'

Lying here dying, I am thinking, he was so right. I was built for so much more. But then, where did I screw it all up. Where?

Love, Lust & Lies

Even if abba was now willing to send me to a school, no school was willing to take me as their student. I appeared for examinations in about a dozen big-small schools, but goes without a doubt, I flunked in all. Abba made out early that exams alone will not help, he needs to do something more. And something more in my town means donation, and donation means bribe, and bribe means a protocol which needs a strict following. All of them said the same, 'Muqarram *sahab*, your son is weak. Of course for you we will try and make an exception. All you need to do is to pay the donation amount and we will be more than happy to have him with us.'

The school demanding least bribe........oh sorry, "least donation" was selected. I was all set to join a school. Kurta-Pajama was replaced by white shirt and grey shorts. Leather slippers by a pair of black shoes. Slate with registers, chalks with pencils and pens.

'Now you look like a true Englishman,' Ammi remarked with the biggest possible smile on her face when I got ready on the first day in my brand new uniform. I thought I was looking like a fool in those shorts. I used to believe that only urchins wear them, who clean tables at small restaurants and keep running around in same shorts for decades. I was a little astonished to learn that kids in schools also wear the same. The zip near the crotch was also very disturbing. Why you need them. Pajamas never had a zip, huh!

We walked to the school with her head held higher than usual. She told me to concentrate on English and make only English speaking friends so that I will pick it up quickly.

We reached the gates. She hugged me and in I went. A little apprehensive, a little timid. And suddenly there was a huge grin on my face. I was glad to see an old friend. Right in front of me was a basket ball court.

Feeling a lot better, next I had to look for my classroom. Over here, unlike a madrasa, there were different classrooms for different standards. I had to search for a while. I located it on the first floor after taking two left turns from the stairs. All this while I noticed huge notice boards on the corridor walls with colorful charts all around. There was a cutout of a laughing joker as well, with his hands in the air. It seemed like he was malevolently laughing at me and saying, "Run away Ameen, you look like my distant cousin and will be pinned to a wall just like I have been." I slapped him tight and entered my class to be surprised once again.

There were tables and chairs for students to sit on. I no more had to sit on the ground. I somewhat forgot about all my apprehensions. I was loving it. I took the last bench in a corner. It was nice to feel my bum on a chair. There was only one more student then in the room as I had come a little early. He kept staring at me for a good five minutes before asking, 'are you a new student out here, a fresher?' I nodded. He asked my name.

'Ameen,' I said.

'Hi, I am Aayush. Which school were you in before this?' Now I was a little surprised to hear that name. I expected an Ali or a Zeeshan or a Zoheb to be honest.

'I was not in a school but in a madrasa. Do you know *Darut Talim Was Sanat*?' He shook his head. 'That's close by. I studied there.'

'So this is the first time you have come to a school?' I nodded. He gave me a cunning smile as if he sniffed out that I was a rube. A well polished rube.

It was time for another shock. A girl entered the class and my jaw dropped open. She was wearing a skirt and a shirt. The

Love, Lust & Lies

site was quite intimidating. I tried not to look at her. *Shameless creatures*, I thought. How one can put legs on show. Soon a few more naked legs walked in making me feel more vulnerable.

A little later a boy walked in and sat right next to a girl. My jaw dropped down, all the way to the floor now. They were talking freely, without any restrictions. Now this was petrifying. There were chances that a girl could come in and sit next to me as well. I picked up my bag from the floor, and kept it on the vacant seat next to me.

Soon the class was full with kids. Some running around for no reason, some talking with their chicks for all the reasons, some flying paper planes, some sitting quietly. There was one thing common in all. They all were staring at me every few seconds. I was feeling like a Martian. I could have fainted any minute now. Thankfully the teacher arrived and everyone settled down, but the surprises kept flowing in. It was a lady teacher. She was wearing a sari, one could see her flat stomach, her navel clearly, and a fat bunch of keys hanging lose, making sounds with every step of hers. This place is full of shameless, brazen characters, I thought. Teachers are going around semi nude, what else you can expect. Huh!

Each and every moron in that room started barking, "Miss, there is a new boy. Miss, there is a new boy." I made a note of the word, 'miss.' She looked around before a few morons pointed me out.

'What is your name *beta*?' Its miss, not maulvi, I reminded myself, '*miss*, Ameen Jalaal.' She then for my sake told everyone to introduce themselves. Probably she was not in a mood to teach, and found an excuse in me. I stood there quietly and one by one all the morons barked their names for me to memorize.

Rohan-Sohan, Mohit-Rohit, Ram-Shyam, Karan-Arjun, Jai-Veeru, Sita-Gita, Ganga-Jamuna. I thought such names existed only in films. At madrasa there was no one who had such names. All new, unique names. *Filmy* names.

There were a few more surprises waiting to come my way. I needed to visit the toilet. I asked miss and went around looking. I was just hoping that the toilets are not the same for boys and girls, and was pleased to find that they were not. I entered and for a minute stood confused. Where the hell do I pee here? Another boy entered and I discreetly stood there, waiting to see where he leaks. And when I saw what he did, all my pee tripped back into my bladder. There was a vessel attached in the wall, he stood and peed in that.

What was that? I was never told that, in a school I will have to urinate in a vessel stuck out of a wall. I had never done it like that before. At home we sit and pee like humans. Dogs pee like that. Baffled, I went back the same. But in an hour or so it became irrepressible. I went back to the toilet, stood in front of the vessel, went forward, unzipped, and there it went. I did it like that for the first time. It was quite scary. I also understood the importance of zip being at the right place.

After the final bell rang, most of the students rushed and sat in a rickety bus parked near the gates. I thought, like the tables and the chairs, a school also provides bus and a home drop facility. I got over excited and rushed in only to be thrown out by the conductor a little later. The conductor showed his tobacco stained teeth, 'you need to pay fees for this, get out.' Not all the best things in the world are for free, I suppose. A little dejected I walked back home.

Somehow the first day at school had got over without any other surprise. I reached the porch of my house. I looked next door and found Zareen standing outside, leaning to a wall, having a piece of melon. I stood there looking at her, transfixed. Juice trickling down the sides of her lips. The strong current of air not

Love, Lust & Lies

powerful enough to make my eyes blink. A little later she noticed me. I went up to her. An uncomfortable silence. I could feel breeze ruffle my hair, making a whistling and a whooshing sound in my ears.

'Hi!' I said.

'Half-pant and shirt. You look good. Madrasa dress changed I suppose.' I was glad she spoke. 'I am no more in a madrasa. I am going to a school.' I was expecting her to be stunned. But her eyes, face, expressions remained the same. Nothing contracted or expanded. I made out that I need to say something to get the old Zareen back. Something which I believed I will never say to her.

'I am sorry Zareen. I am really sorry for I didn't turn up that day to save......' That was enough. She smiled. I felt much comfortable, much better. Can you beat that? Comfortable not after boasting or after throwing my weight around Zareen, but in-fact after apologizing. My friend was back again.

Technology all my life surprised me. Virus, anti- virus, nuclear bombs, space ships, all were brilliant inventions. But these things hardly ever made a difference to our town's day-to-day life. But there was one invention which changed everyone in the town. That was coming of satellite television channels. Cable TV. A person who used to sit in front of television screen for an hour a day, was now glued to it all day long. And why not? We had one channel earlier, but now there were more channels than the television set could register. Zee TV, Star TV, Sony TV, Movie channels, sports channels. Television set actually became a little jungle in itself where one could easily get lost. Doordarshan was suddenly out of the game. *Alif Laila* and *Chandra Kanta* were no more gracing our screens. Ammi's new favorite shows were *Parampara* and *Banegi apni baat.*

Things were changing. I can say that because there were changes not only in the television world, but also in my subjects. There was suddenly a 'history' in which they told me that there were kings and queens in India 300 years ago. There was geography, in which I saw the map for the first time and discovered that there are so many countries and there is more water than land on earth. There was Science, where I learnt that trees have life and leaves are their kitchen. There was Mathematics, which I suppose no one liked. There was Hindi language and of course, English.

Initially I faced problems as all the subjects were in English language. But I picked it up soon. Credit need not be given to me but to my great ammi. She made out quick that for me to understand all that assorted stuff is as difficult as selling ice to an Eskimo. I needed a personal tutor. All she had to do was to have a small fight with abba to get his approval. Soon, every evening five to six I was sitting with a certain Mr. Gupta. A man in his thirties, with thousands of tiny holes on his face, as if someone poked his face with a pencil a thousand times mercilessly.

At school, as expected all snubbed me in the beginning. They discovered my worth on the basketball court. The game was still new for most of them. If there was anything that I learnt in madrasa which was going to help me here, was basketball. I need to thank that scoundrel minister for this. I promised that after I turn eighteen I will vote at least once for that bastard. But only once. I can't forgive him for the burning hot sun he made us sit under.

Usually I was never selected in any of the teams my class mates used to form. One day a guy fell short and I got my big break. I seized it with both hands. Lay-up shot, dribbling, three pointers, free throws, I was better than their best. I suddenly

Love, Lust & Lies

became important. I wanted to be on the court as much as possible.

One of my basketball buddies was Karan Sahay. A short guy whose ammi had instructed him to play the game so that his height would increase. But Karan was short only of height, not ideas, especially weird ideas.

He told me to watch a show called Baywatch on TV where one can give a treat to their eyes. There are many sexy girls, in skimpy outfits, completely drenched in water. As white as milk. He added that if one is lucky, he might get to see a kiss as well.

'Lip to Lip. Not on the cheeks or forehead like our sad Indian heroes. That show is a must watch. Don't miss it Ameen.' Primarily I ignored his advice. Why should I watch such insane and cheap stuff. But to learn that there are people kissing on the lips was quite intriguing and intimidating at the same time. I gave it another thought.

Should I watch? *'No!'* May be I must watch! *'Ahhhhnnn!'*
I must watch, all my friends do so. *'Yes!'*
What if abba ammi catch me? *'Forget It!'*
I had somewhat started to settle down in my school.

Possibly abba was the one who was drawing maximum returns due to the coming of cable TV. He could listen to his news 24x7, as there were a few channels now dedicated solely for this purpose. A proper democracy needs a good media support. This boom somewhat helped to keep a tab on corruption through sting operations. The first name which comes to my head is of Tarun Tejpal and his "Tehelka" team.

Those days they were talking about Vajpayee's bus to Lahore, which ironically was followed by the Kargil war. Army General Parvez Musharraf soon was the president of Pakistan, while George Bush the new American president. They also talked about Kargil coffin purchase scandal, Ketan Parekh scam and the Orissa cyclones. On television, Movers and Shakers made news while Karan Johar, a young film director was being appreciated.

I was probably big now and I can say that for two reasons. One, because I could understand most of the things they mentioned on the news, and two, because abba told me so one day.

'Ameen, you are a big boy now. You can understand things, can eat on your own, sleep alone, read and write. You are doing so much to do well in *this* world. A world which is temporary. A life which is full of illusions. How are you preparing yourself for the *real* world. The life after death. On the judgment day when you will be questioned, you will shake your head like an idiot. How will you face the almighty. Will you say, "No I did nothing for you almighty. I was busy learning a foreign tongue and a stupid game called Basketball." You will be whipped and burnt in the fire of hell. So from now on, you should offer namaaz five times in a day. I hope you keep that in your head.'

This namaaz instruction didn't come down as a surprise. I knew abba would say that someday. I knew that someday I have to start. If it makes everyone feel that I am big enough, why not? I nodded and I felt 'big enough.'

Abba's golden diary though had somewhat a different explanation for growing up. It said:
"A child grows up when he realizes that he has the right not only to be right, but also to be wrong."

I was not sure if I had reached that stage yet, but yes, I could sense that it was near. I was somewhere in between, I guess. Neither a child, nor an adult. But I guess I was more of an adult, as I never cared a jack for abba's strict instruction of praying five times a day. I had somewhat realized that I had the right to be wrong.

Love, Lust & Lies

"Dreams create realities - through hard work."
Whoever said this looked into life deeply.

I understood this when finally after years of sweating out, perseverance, and savings, abba today realized his dream. Probably the only dream he ever saw with his eyes wide open. He bought a car. A sizzling red Maruti 800. He was the happiest person in the world that day.

Abba parked the car and we checked it out for hours. I took the driver's seat and kept on fidgeting with the steering. Every passerby came in and congratulated abba. Everyone loved the car, and even if there was someone who didn't like it, was courteous enough to manipulate his statement well.

We all deserved a treat and abba didn't let the gleeful moment pass away starkly. We all went for a ride around the town. Zareen also hopped in. Ammi took the front seat while we sat in the rear. It was funny to see ammi sitting with her face covered in the car as well. Abba smiled and told her to remove it for some time. She did the same.

The very next moment she scooped her face out of the window, allowing the gush of wind slap her face. It was one of those moments you want your life to freeze at. Everything was so perfect. Abba had his car, ammi had her freedom and Zareen was next to me.

It was expected from everyone to carry a pre-conceived notion in their heads that the attitude of our family would change as we own a car now. To be honest, it happened on the contrary. Everyone else's attitude towards our family changed. More aliens and hardly familiar faces started visiting us, more aunties were cooking delicacies and sending it over. In the meantime, gossipmongers found a new topic for discussion and were doing their job quite well, i.e. bitching behind our backs. We very much remained the same.

On the personal front I had to face a few small problems. It was a little too much for a few kids at school to see me arrive in a car. I don't know exactly if it was insecurity, jealousy, or for sheer fun. But a rough guess says that it was a mix of the three. Insecure, as I may get a little more attention of the girls, jealous as their abbas were not rich or hardworking enough to buy one, and fun part I don't need to explain.

Eventually I earned a sobriquet. Someone had seen abba dropping me and smeared, 'Every morning there comes a *daadhi* in a *gaadhi*. A maulvi who turned a car driver. You people must have a *dekko*.' All the morons used to laugh. Falling on their chicks, holding their tummies, they would laugh. Sometimes I myself used to find it quite amusing, '*gaadhi mein dadhi.*' I pondered over it when alone, and felt that you need an extremely creative head to coin a term like that.

Otherwise, my school was going great. I was now a known figure, courtesy; Basketball. Studies were going just fine, except for mathematics. Actually I was looking for a certain Pythagoras who discovered the so called Pythagoras theorem. I swear, the way this man has tortured the students even after his death, no one else comes a close second. There were a few other scientists and theorists who are a member of the same gang, but their names were so difficult that I was never able to retain them.

If I die tonight and meet 'Pythagoras, the Python' up there, I would definitely tell him that he was a bozo and not some creative jerk. But only if I die tonight. Let's see.

Life was moving on comfortably for me, but I could sense a lot had changed in Zareen's life. It had almost come to a standstill. She was also a black haunted figure now, as she had to go around in a veil. She no more used to skip the rope with me, neither used to run behind and hold the berry eating competition or scare the squirrels. In fact, everything we used to do together outside in the open suddenly stopped. We were still allowed to play carom and ludo indoor. I was a bit confused by this 'inside-allowed, outside-not allowed' stuff. I asked her why she can't play outside or run around her house with me like before. She nonchalantly replied that her ammi ordered this as she was a grown up girl now.

The picture was still hazy and her answer made me more curious. So next, I went to ammi and posed the same question.

Ammi gave a sigh and explained, 'life of girls come to a halt very soon Ameen. They are preserved like biscuits in hermetic jars. A boy will always be told that his reach should exceed his grasp to make it to the heavens. While a girl's limbs will be amputated early so that she can never dare to exceed her grasp. The heavens are only meant for boys I guess.'

She took a small breather. I could not follow every part of her speech, but it was good enough to get the picture. She continued, 'but people will never say it that way. They will manipulate it all, cut it short and make it sound pleasant by saying that, 'girls grow up very quickly.'

She stopped and played again, 'Girls don't live all days of their lives Ameen. I just wish and pray that some day when the sun will rise, all the girls in the world will live all the days of their lives. The god who gave us life forgot to give us freedom.'

There was some sort of concealed pain in her lines. A pain of her own life.

On television, an old retired actor was hosting a reality show called, 'Kaun Banega Crorepati.' Ammi when saw the show while swapping channels exclaimed, 'oh, he is back.' I didn't know who she was talking about. 'That's Amitabh Bachchan. He was a big star once. He looks so old now. How time flies by.' Eventually that show went on to become a huge hit and Bachchan was suddenly everywhere.

But ammi was not a very big fan of the *Crorepati* show. Like all other women in India, may it be the ones who wear a veil or run around naked, who bitch or don't bitch, were watching 'Kyunki Saas Bhi Bahu Thi'. It became so popular that the makers launched many such shows one after the other. The USP of all these shows were confused characters, glycerin, rebirths, plastic surgeries and alphabet 'K.' These shows also hold the honor of being the biggest reason for the agony of many males in India. On many occasions abba wanted to watch news, ammi wouldn't allow him to do so and he would comment, 'by watching you women going mad for such shows, I truly agree with the men who said that women will be the last thing civilized by man.'

And when ammi was done, the news reporters would start blabbering. It was good in a way as I became more aware of things happening around. There was an earthquake in Gujarat on the Republic day, Anil Kumble took a perfect ten against Pakistan, Nepal royal family massacre, Hrithik Roshan the star was born, two extremely great men, Madhav Rao Scindia and Dhirubhai Ambani were no more.

But there was one event that had a huge impact. This event was 9/11. Two planes went into two American towers and they came tumbling down. The Americans went mad and blamed it all on a lanky man called Osama Bin Laden and bombed Afghanistan. The irony was, they killed everyone in Afghanistan but Osama Bin Laden. While there were rumors that their own government was behind these attacks. Who so ever did it, the attackers still remain mysterious till date.

Back home in India, there was one event which left its mark. The *Godhra* riots. Some Hindu pilgrims were allegedly burnt alive in a rail coach by a five hundred strong Muslim crowd. This was followed by communal riots, leaving more than 1000 people all over India dead. But the state of Gujarat was the worst hit. Muslims were butchered in that state, woman raped and children charred. What disturbing was to see the officials turning blind eye towards the massacre. Narendra Modi, the chief minister of Gujarat became an overnight star.

I don't know if world is the same place after 9/11, but I can say one thing for sure, the world is no more the same for Muslims. It changed. It became difficult.

Abba had somehow managed to erase Babri, but Godhra revived everything. He was disturbed. That day we both were walking towards the mosque for our evening prayers. On our way used to fall a temple. I had always seen the temple priest and him exchanging hellos. That day they didn't.

There were two dogs loitering outside the temple. Abba commented, 'dogs will live with dogs off course, huh!' We continued moving and reached the mosque. And guess what? There were three dogs loitering outside the mosque. I caught abba looking at me sheepishly. He suddenly picked up a small bamboo from the ground and ran like a cynic behind the dogs. He had lost it.

Godhra, Bush, Afghanistan, Osama and all the news related to these words had affected abba on a ground scale. He was suddenly doing this Hindu-Muslim thing in every other stuff.

A movie called Lagaan won an Oscar nomination for itself. Abba beamed and said, 'Only a Muslim could have done that, and Aamir Khan did it.'

Ammi loved to tease him on these topics. She quipped, 'But Mother India went for Oscars much earlier. And if I remember correctly, it had Sunil Dutt.'

'So what? The lead role was of Nargis, and the filmmaker was Mehboob Khan,' Abba said proudly. He didn't stop there. Forget the Oscars, the biggest star this country ever saw was a Muslim. Dilip Kumar. In fact, even the biggest villain, Gabbar Singh, was also played by a Muslim man, Amjad Ali Khan. Even the most beautiful heroines were Madhubala, Parveen Babi, Zeenat Amaan. All Muslims again.

It was quite amusing and comical to learn that abba also used to check out girls once upon a time. But more than that I wondered what kind of Muslim names they had. Kumars and Madhubalas. He cleared the air, 'Dilip is Yusuf Khan, while Madhubala was Mumtaz Begum Jehan.'

Ammi again poked him, 'but you are forgetting one star in between. If I remember he was your favorite as well. And in front of him all these Khans and Kumars of yours look sloppy.'

Abba and I intently looked at her to know who is this Super-Man she is talking about.

'Amitabh Bachchan. Now please don't present a rebuttal for that. You will sound foolish. And by the way, he is making a comeback. Tell your Khans and Kumars to buckle up.' Abba really found it difficult to refute that. However, he found a way out.

'But then, who made Bachchan? Salim-Javed. All his movies were written by the duo. You name it. Be it Sholay, Zanjeer, Deewar, Don etc. etc. The minds behind his great movies

Love, Lust & Lies

were Muslim minds.' Ammi retaliated, 'that's not fair. You were talking about actors. You fight on some topic and switch over to some other.'

They continued like kids and I don't know if abba ever stopped talking like a fanatic. But I realized one important thing that day. Thankfully, early in life.

You can be a Ram, or a Rahim, or a Rafael, or a Rosario, or anyone for that matter of fact, and yet be happy and successful. Be it spiritual success, material success or anything you are looking for. One's religion, name, color, cast, creed, simply doesn't count. It is you and your commitment, your preferences, your choices, your destiny and your power to imagine things which makes you or breaks you. God has given everyone enough and equal fuel to go out there like fire and take on the whole world.

If this isn't true then Dilip Kumar should have been a disaster for he changed his name, Mohammed Ali whose real name is Cassius Clay should have died in some shanty in America. If you are born in a Brahmin family and if your neighbor in a Shudra, it doesn't make you more intelligent than him. As I said, it all depends on you. We all need to discover the power in you.

Believe, have faith, but don't set your preferences or considerations on the basis of religion. Different religions will show you different roads to lead a happy and a contented life. But all the roads end at the same destination. How should it matter then? God has no religion I suppose.

Garrison Keillor gets it right somewhat when he says this-:

"Anyone who thinks that sitting in a church can make you a Christian, must also think that sitting in a garage can make you a car."

One of the best stories I ever read was by Billy Watterson. At the end of this story, he asks a very-very interesting question. Here it goes-:

It's the Christmas evening. Two friends, Calvin and Hobbes are talking over a can of beer-;

CALVIN:
This whole Santa Claus thing just doesn't make sense. Why all the secrecy? Why all the mystery?
If the guy exists, why doesn't he ever show himself and prove it?
And if he doesn't exist what's the meaning of all this?
HOBBES:
I don't know. By the way, isn't this a religious holiday?
CALVIN:
Yeah, but actually, I've got the same questions about God."

I found out *my* answer later in life and I hope everyone finds it out for themselves. It makes your life easier to lead.

Trust Me!

I can never forget that day. Everything is crystal clear. When I was slapped, boxed and bruised for the first time in my life. It all started on the place I loved to hang around the most. The basketball court. To say that it was a close game going on, will be an understatement. Absolute neck to neck. As usual, I was the key player. Rohan dribbled the ball into our half and could have scored the all important basket if I hadn't snatched it at the eleventh hour from him. I covered ground and a lay-up shot did it for my team. I turned around and self-patronizingly announced, 'you might be the next best thing Rohan, but not quite me dude.'

Rohan was a well built guy. Tall and broad with a tiny mole on his right cheek. But when it came to basketball, he sucked. One weird thing about bullies is, that they want to have their way in everything. Even at things they suck. We won the game and he was furious. More so because of my line which was well directed at him and that too in public.

On my way back home I used to cross a secluded alley, similar to the one in which I waited years before for Zareen to turn up for the movie. But that day someone was waiting for me. One doesn't need to think hard. It was Rohan.

'Don't you think that you were acting a little too smart today at the courts.' I remained quiet. Still a bit surprised to find him there. He came forward and pasted a thundering slap on my right cheek and then pulled my hair with enormous power.

'How many times I need to tell people not to rub me the wrong way.' Then he pushed his face inside my ear. I could feel his wet lips all over on the flap of my ear. He yelled as loud as any man is capable of, *"Bloody Mullah."* The words went in from one ear, ripped my drums apart and came out from the other. I lost the little control I had on myself. He boxed my right eye several times, not stopping before it turned black & blue. Soon I was on the floor. Rohan didn't stop. He broke my right knee with his shoe heel. I roared in pain, but nobody turned up. He left me lying there half dead for another half an hour before some good Samaritan noticed and carried me to the nearest nursing home.

Soon abba-ammi were there. It all ended with five stitches under my eye and a fractured knee. The doctor instructed me to stay in for four weeks and not to run around for at least three months. We went back home. Everyone was quiet. I was expecting them to bombard me with questions, but till now no questions erupted out of anyone's mouth. They were aghast to see me in such a condition. Nevertheless, I appreciated their silence.

For the next four weeks all I did was to look at the ceiling, try to count the number of times a fan rotates in a minute, see how the tungsten burns in a bulb and pretense to read course books. But most of the time I thought of creative ways of killing Rohan?

Soon the question which was procrastinated for several days was posed by abba, 'what happened that day? Who did this to you?' I knew the answer. I had rehearsed it several times. But trust me, when the moment arrives, nothing works. You forget it all.

'Err…ah, abba… I won a basketball game and…and a boy didn't like it and……………' I went quiet after that. Anyways, that was enough for him. He left the room. He looked miserable.

One day while standing in front of the mirror I realized that there were furs coming out of my once smooth cheeks. Small particles, like moss on stone that pops out in rains. The first glimpse of what will be a beard soon. It reminded me of Rohan. His curse words, "Mullah. *Bloody* Mullah."

Four weeks flew by and I returned to school. To be flabbergasted that everyone knew about the ugly episode. I made it out because I could see that lecherous smile on many a faces. It blew me over when I overheard a few of them maliciously using the word 'mullah.'

I was still on my crutches, and now, I desperately wanted to see Rohan as well hopping around with them. I knew I had to think of something out of the box. If I really wanted to nail Rohan, I needed to take help from an equally bastard guy. There was only one name ringing in my head again and again. But I was a bit apprehensive as it was years I met him last. Thankfully, apprehension fell small in front of my frustration that day. I decided to meet Zain.

I wanted to make my bumping into Zain look like an accident and thus instead of going to his house, I went to the mosque, he visits every Friday. The same mosque we had flicked the umbrellas from. I wanted to re-unite the umbrella flickers.

If you ever had an opportunity of visiting a mosque on a Friday, you will know how difficult it is to find an appropriate place to sit comfortably, and today I was here to find someone. It was no less than trying to find a needle somewhere hidden prudently in a haystack. The crutches were not making things any easier either. I reached earlier and took a seat on the terrace. The terrace of a mosque on Fridays is a hangout for the people who just come for the heck of coming to a mosque. They don't need to listen to the imam as the mikes on the terrace hardly work. I was pretty sure that Zain will be spotted somewhere here. An hour went by, but no sign of him. I started feeling vulnerable. Every kurta-pajama and cap clad man that entered had my eyes on him. I peeped down from the window and could see nothing except a herd of similar people sitting on mats, looking lost somewhere.

I went down and ran my eyes around, but no sign of him. I started panicking. I wanted to see him badly. I could get a quaint view of the imam who was speaking in a very animated fashion about the ways to impress the almighty. I stood there for a while but he was seen nowhere. I decided to go to the *wazu-khana* or the place where people wash their hands and feet. I reached there, supported my crutches against the wall and sat on one of the benches. I splashed my face hard with water. Someone suddenly tapped my right shoulder, I turned around and saw someone holding my crutches. He said, 'they fell, here take it.' I looked up and can you believe it who that was?

Zain was standing right in front of me. By no ways or means I could believe my eyes. Shell shocked. It was like a dream actually. He was much taller, stronger, broader and fatter than before. I still sat there looking at him, unaware of the running tap behind. He looked at me for a couple of seconds, a little perplexed at my gaze and gape. And then he recognized me, 'Ameen. You are Ameen.' I gladly nodded. And my gladness had no limits when I noticed a smile on his face. We hugged each other. I don't know if that thing on my cheek was a drop of water or a tear, but if I had to bet, I would say it was a drop of tear.

After the namaaz, we met outside. After the formal questions, he finally asked what I was here to answer.

'What happened, how you fractured your leg?' Without wasting even a millisecond I barked the whole story out. When I was done, I didn't have to plead like, "Oh Zain, please break Rohan's leg."

'Where can I find him,' was all that Zain said.

The plan was set. I had to somehow get Rohan to the same alley. Zain promised he will take it forward from there. I was still facing a few problems with my leg, thus decided to see him after a few weeks. I was waiting with a bated breath for that day. Though

Rohan was bulky, he was nothing in front of Zain. I was bloody sure that Zain would beat the shit out of him.

I somehow had to remain patient till my legs were good enough to sprint a few five hundred meters. Every day I would try to run, the knee would hurt and I would stop with a jerk. The wait was looking long and time very difficult to kill. I decided to keep myself busy.

I began to learn driving. Abba happily agreed and every day after the school he would reveal the secrets of the clutch, the gear and the accelerator. I say secrets because you know how dramatic abba can be. I also learnt cooking. Zareen used to cook some great bake fish. So the evenings were killed in her kitchen, playing with pans and bowls. Soon I could drive a car, cook baked fish and *run as before.*

The first thing I did after realizing that my legs can break into a dash was, to go and see Zain. The following day was finalized to slay Rohan.

The last bell at school was about to ring. It all looked like the day I had thrown the paper ball when Zain had to woo Rubina. I was so scared that day. It all looked as if an action replay was about to take place. At times, I wanted to back off, thinking that Rohan will get the better of Zain, or worse, Zain wouldn't turn up. But the desire in me to see that bastard stuttering around with crutches in his hands kept me going. I kept adding fuel to the fire within me which was going lull at times.

Ding Ding Ding Ding........It was time. I came out. Rohan was standing near the gate with a bunch of ass-lickers. I went straight to him and stood in his face. Stared, and slapped him in full public glare. It stuck well. I know this because the sound was mesmerizing. Before he could make out what had happened, I was long gone. Right then and there he made the biggest mistake of his life. He ran behind me. I could see him chasing me. I could smell him now. I almost gave up. 'No Ameen! You can't get caught. Run Ameen run.' My knees showed signs of tearing down. My brain showed signs of wooziness. And then I saw the lane. I was almost there. Almost, almost, almo... when Rohan caught hold of my shirt collar. I knew I was dead.

But do you know what happens when god leads you to the edge? Either he teaches you how to fly. Or he catches you when you are about to fall. And he definitely did catch me well that evening.

I had made it to the entrance of the lane. It was quite bizarre, or I would say, a quintessential Hindi film scene. For Zain made an entry exactly when Rohan was holding me by my collars and was about to box me. Zain blocked his punch, held the asshole's right hand and twisted it swiftly. He shrieked in pain. I heard some of his bones crack. My ears loved that crunching sound. Zain kept his right hand twisted, and continued boxing his right eye till it started throwing blood.

Rohan was now lying there like a fish freshly taken out of a pond. Watching him in that pain should have cooled me a bit. But on the contrary, I felt more powerful than this six footer. It provoked me to do more.

Zain sat next to him, kneeled on the ground. He took out a cigarette pack.

'Care for one?' He asked. I shook my head. He took out a matchbox and with a flick of a matchstick against the box lit the tip of his cigarette stick. It struck an ugly idea in my head. I came forward and took the cigarette from Zain. I kneeled down next to Rohan. Smoke of tobacco filled my nostrils. He was still in pain, holding his eye. I gazed at his mole on the right cheek for a good two minutes. I went in his ears, bit the flap and said, 'let's get a mole on your left cheek as well. A *bigger* one.'

I dipped the burning end into his cheek. He yelled and yelled and yelled. I was filled with bliss, more bliss and more bliss. I loved it. I dipped it again. He yelled again. I started loving this game. This all dipping-yelling game. I was about to burn him again when Zain held my hand.

'Enough Ameen! Let's leave!'

We walked till the market circle. From there, Zain had to take a different turn for his house. I hugged him tight.

'Thank you for being a true friend! Thanks a ton brother,' I said.

'Till the time you will keep flicking umbrellas for me, I will keep bashing up guys for you.'

I watched him go and realized that although I had been a tad selfish, and never ever after madrasa stayed in touch with Zain, he at once agreed to help me. He exemplified the definition which says that "friends are like stars. You may not see them, but be sure that they are always there, and when it will be dark, they will be back."

If you were born in India I am sure you would have come across a theory which holds guests equivalent to gods. I am sorry, but it's false and a lie. I don't buy this jazz. And if guests are like gods, then I prefer to follow Satan. Because the guests who were occupying my house for the last two days and were going to be here for the next five days were nothing more but a bunch of swindlers.

My abba had a long list of relatives. Which all his life he had boasted off. Talk about any city in the world and he would figure out some daughter of his nephew whose aunt is staying there. Or some long lost brother or someone else. Now one fine day, or rather I would say, that ill-omened day, one of abba's relatives came over to our town from Bombay.

They were three of them. With three very unique noses. Kashif, whom I had to involuntarily call Kashif *uncle*, had a long nose like Pinocchio. Khurshid, whom I had to involuntarily call Khurshid *aunty* had a round and a plump nose with a nose ring as big as a cycles tyre dangling around. And Rehan, sixteen something, with possibly the biggest nose I ever saw on any boy's face. My god, it was something. Just like a woodpecker is master at picking wood, he was a master at picking nose. I named him 'the nose-pecker.'

Now because guests are considered gods in this part of the world, it was my duty along with abba ammi to treat them like one. In order to please gods you make a lot of sacrifices. Therefore in order to please these junky gods, I was made the sacrificial goat.

'Ameen, Rehan wants to go to the market. Please go with him.'

'Ameen, Kashif uncle wants to eat *jalebi*, please get some.'

'Ameen, Khurshid aunty forgot where is the loo. Please show her.' Can you beat that? She forgot the *loo*.

I had to answer every call like a pet dog that runs when his master whistles. I had to wag my tail, drop my tongue and like the animal that runs behind a Frisbee a million times without showing any displeasure, I had to run around the house and the town.

But the reason which left me irate was that I had to give my room to the nose-pecker and his family. And I had to sleep in the backyard porch. No roof over my head and I ended up in a delicious meal for the mosquitoes. The other reason was that in every line they had to mention their city, Bombay. And everyone was quite impressed.

Love, Lust & Lies

Day in and day out the nose-pecker and his family would eat and yak about Bombay.

'Oh, some or the other movie star is always passing by. The roads are bustling with a fleet of cars. It's not like your town where roads are meant for cows and dogs. It's all organized. There are tall buildings and then there are very tall buildings.' Now whatever he meant by that, not a single proton, neutron or even the moron in my body was interested.

Listening to their continuous blabbering was a torment. I sometimes wanted to smoke a few cigarettes. Zain said it alleviates frustration. My board exams were inching closer, but because of these bozos, I was hardly getting any time to study. Though I was never a nerd, my preparations were nil till now. Yet I was apprehensive because when its high school, every ammi in town will call my ammi and ask cattily, "how much did Ameen score Najma?"

That evening we all were sitting in the living room when Kashif, "the Pinocchio nosed asked," 'so Ameen, what are your plans after school?' Now that was bloody stupid of Kashif to ask such a question. Or maybe he wanted to embarrass me. In towns, no kid plans his future. They simply wait for their parents to instruct them. Parents decide whether you should sit in the small shop they own and sell duplicate biscuits and adulterate sacks or look after the hens and cocks and collect their eggs and excreta.

I remained mum and Pinocchio continued, 'well, Rehan is going to study commerce and will later do MBA and be a manager in some MNC.' He proudly showed all his thirty-two well tanned yellow teeth. While nose-pecker smiled coyly with a finger well placed in his nose. Suddenly Kashif got excited, 'why don't you come over to Bombay after high school. You can take admission in Rehan's school. Finding a place to stay is not difficult in Bombay. Half of the city is made up of people who have come there from other similar small towns. What do you think Ameen?' I didn't know what to say. I rolled my eyeballs towards abba. Pinocchio was much intelligent than I thought. He understood I was not the boss. He asked again, 'what do you think Muqarram?' I was pretty sure that abba would turn the idea down in no minute. But it was time for the shocker of shockers. 'Sounds interesting. Let's see after his results are out.'

I instantly developed a soft corner for Pinocchio and nose-pecker. Suddenly, every word about Bombay seemed wonderful and true. Tall buildings, big roads, organized city, beaches. I was reveling in my own world. I was so happy that I took the nose pecker on an all paid movie trip. He promised return of favor once I come over to Bombay.

A few days later the nose pecker and his family left. Pinocchio just before taking the train at the station told abba, "Look Muqarram, there are so many educated and talented people in towns and small villages. What happens with them in the end? They all die in the same village after a *miserable* life. Why? Because they don't get the proper opportunities and guidance to explore their potential. Ameen is an educated young man now. Don't waste him. Send him out of this mess. Send him out of the jungles to the city. Bombay will give him loads of opportunity to learn and excel. It's not called the city of dreams for no reason. Just give me a ring and I will be more than happy to help with his admissions.'

The train whizzed past us. I kept looking at the last bogie and the 'X' mark on its rear till I lost its sight. If things go well then soon I will also be on board of this train and chug past all the small towns, and then very small villages as Pinocchio mentioned, en route to the biggest city of our country, 'Bombay.' The lines of Pinocchio held our town in bad light. He used words like mess and jungle to describe it. It did hit abba, I could see it in his eyes, but somewhere deep down his heart, he knew that Pinocchio had shown him the mirror. If he called weed a weed and not a flower, he didn't do any wrong.

Soon my board exams happened. We were waiting for the results. Abba's news channels were telling him numerous things. They were talking about an Iraqi man called Saddam Hussein who was about to be hanged. He had troubled the American president a lot, and he was having his revenge. The Abdul Karim Telgi scam came to the fore. Irfan Pathan was the new cricket sensation. On TV, Jassi was the new star and Indian Idol the new favorite show. One of the biggest dacoits of modern India, Veerappan was finally gunned down. Columbia air crashed wherein Kalpana Chawla, an Indian lady astronaut lost her life in space.

And then one day a news flash read; 'CBSE board: tenth class results out.' It meant that I had completed my high school. I didn't score very high marks, but good enough and way above my own expectations. I was biting my nails, thinking all day long if abba was really serious about sending me to Bombay

And then one day abba called me and asked, 'Do you want to go to *Bum-bay-ee*?' With that one question abba defied the rules of a town. He was asking his *son* what he wanted to do. I didn't know how to react. I turned a drone. Overwhelmed by the importance showered. Ammi in the background was looking carefully, waiting transfixed for my reply. I said a very meek 'yes'. I noticed that the eyes of all three of us were brimming with fresh tears. Proud eyes. Hopeful eyes.

Abba made a call to Pinocchio and told him that he will send all my certificates that are required for the admission. In a few days I will be leaving for Bombay. The whole town was soon abuzz with talks that Muqarram's son will be going to Bombay for higher education. Nobody in my family gave a damn to their reactions. Ammi abba wanted me to see the world, learn and rise.

A day or two before my departure, ammi was busy packing my stuff. Every small article, right from toothbrush to the corner in which my comb was stuffed was told to me shed-load of times. I noticed she was doing all that with downcast eyes. A little downhearted.

'Ammi, are you not happy?' I asked her when she dropped a pair of trousers in the bag.

'Why should I say? You are robbing me of my only vacation?' She looked up, placed her soft hands on my cheek, 'but I don't mind giving it up for your future. I am very happy.'

I went through a similar emotional outburst when I met Zareen that evening. Speaking self-incriminatingly, she kept on demeaning herself.

'I feel, may be from now on you would not like to talk to me or meet me. After all which educated man would like to be in the company of a rustic yokel. An illiterate village girl.' I kept looking at a few stars which had come out a little early. She continued, 'a boy who went to a madrasa, then to a school and now will be attending a college in Bombay. And a girl who swept her house in her small town all her life, together, will raise too many eyebrows.' I was still looking at the sky. The number of stars huge now. I asked her, 'Zareen, can you count the number of stars up in the sky?' Startled by my irrational question she looked at me. I added, 'I know you can't. But you know what the irony is. This big scholar sitting next to you can't count them either.' She smiled which soon was accompanied by tears trickling down her cheeks. I kept my hand on hers. We sat there like that till the whole sky was filled with innumerous stars. I had just then touched a girl for the first time.

　　　　　　　　　　Love, Lust & Lies

Finally the D-day arrived. Luggage rolled in the Maruti, we headed for the railway station. The train to Bombay was waiting on the tracks, as if just for me. I kept on holding ammi's hand. Abba bought a water bottle and a few packets of chips. Ammi was quiet like never before. Abba then took out a packet. Very carefully taped, sealed and packed. His hands holding them came forward, 'here, take this. This is the golden diary. I feel, you are big enough to learn from the intelligent lines I preserved between the two covers.' I didn't feel very nice about this. That diary had been abba's best friend for so many years. But he insisted, and the diary came on board.

The engine whistled. The shrill sound brought me out of my dream. I realized I was going to Bombay for real. I suddenly became nervous. I was going out in the cold, all alone. The sense of excitement stuffed itself somewhere prudently. And the train moved. Ammi walked a couple of steps till abba held her from her shoulders. I kept looking at them from between the window grills. Ammi turned into a black spot, her veil shining, and abba's skull cap intact. Soon their silhouette vanished somewhere. The roads from here on were to be traveled alone. Less Ammi, less abba, and less Zareen.

I was thankful to the almighty that he fulfilled my wish. I got what I laid my heart on. I got it because I asked for it. And asking is the beginning of receiving. Be prepared for it. Make sure you don't go to the ocean with a teaspoon. At least take a bucket so that the kids won't laugh at you. Because at the end, you *will* get it.

If I have to mark this part of my life, I would say it all started here. Most of *the* most wild and crazy incidences of my life transpired in this city. It's Bombay where the story actually begins.

"Fear not thy life shall come to an end, but rather fear that it shall never have a beginning."

My life just now took off.

8th

Before I start telling you all about Bombay, I need to talk about my two day train journey to this magnum opus city. In the true sense of word, my journey into life had begun. And from here on, it's kind of a travelogue.

The train coach was full of all sweaty-smelly people who looked like they haven't shaved since India got independent. Horrendous experience it was, for I had never in my life thought that a train journey can be so big a pain in the ass. There were people everywhere. Every inch of the bogie was utilized to the core. There were people on the birth, below the birth. In the narrow alley given to walk, they sat on their suitcases and even on duffel bags. Cycles were tied tight to the window grills, and there were people sitting on the rooftops as well. Most of the time they sleep with their cheeks on their palms and get up only to have a cigarette discreetly in the yucky toilets, or to buy and eat the absolutely stale food being sold around. Then fart and sleep again.

All around me, going to Bombay like me, to make a fresh beginning were people like these. A second class bogie of Indian railways is also a place where one can learn hell lot of things.

I had the lower birth. I don't know if Nehru passed a bill in the parliament or Gandhi said this in one of his *andolan* speeches, that the lower birth is to be shared with every damn traveler in the train who is carrying an unconfirmed ticket. Why and how the fuck do they get in the train when they don't have a proper ticket? There is an inside story to this.

What happens is, when you don't get a confirmed ticket, all you need to do is to get into the train with a fat wallet, eat peanuts and wait for the ticket checker. It is understood that all the ticket checkers in this country are corrupted and go around with a tattoo stamped on their foreheads which shouts, *"for sale."*

When one of these rogues in a black coat comes over and asks you for a ticket, you simply stuff his crooked ass with a wad of notes. He would then either sell the seat that has been allotted to him and he himself will sit outside a toilet killing mosquitoes. Or will carry out some other scam to make you comfortable.

But these people are not to be solely held responsible for this sleazy act of theirs. If you till now believed that the families of these so called govt. servants run on their pint-sized, petite salaries. Then I am sorry, you got it so wrong. It's on the *bribe*, the money they opt to take, and sleep outside the toilet bearing the shitty stench. In fact, this holds true for all the so called govt. servants of our country. They all run their families similarly. And in Bombay, I will let you meet many such gross characters in my flashback. Let's move on. Let me see where I am.

All right! My train entered the biggest railway station of this country. One of the gems of British architecture, 'The Victoria Terminus.' Abba had informed Pinocchio about my arrival well in advance, but he didn't care enough to be on time to receive me. I stood at the platform stranded. The crowds didn't even stop to give me a wistful glance. All were rushing by in a frenzy of their own. A few yards away from me, a couple was giving a tongue lashing, abusing the poor coolie for demanding an enormous amount for his hard work. He kindly took it all, but ultimately got the amount he wanted. He kept the wad of notes in his pajama, turned away and then gave a whimsical smile. He took the lashing, but got the money.

At the tea stall, vendor poured glasses after glasses, non-stop. In seconds a hand would emerge on the counter and the tea would go down the throat the very next minute. It all happens quickly. The whole station looked in what you can call a quick-quick mode. Fast forward mode kind of.

The first colors of Bombay. They don't walk, jog or trot here. No one can afford to sleep walk here. You *need to, need to* sprint, gallop, dash, and like others, be in a frenzy of your own. Be a little selfish, a little self centered, a little venal like a mercenary. It doesn't matter.

After taking their own sweet time, Pinocchio and nose pecker arrived, acting as if they were helluva busy. We hailed a black & yellow cab and went to his house near Andheri station. I was probably expecting a lot from Bombay, because the first impression of the city was pathetic. Open drains, uncontrolled traffic, mad beggars, innumerable people, all going against the rosy picture I was carrying in my mind.

When the cab finally pulled up outside Pinocchio's shanty, Khurshid was there at the door. I could read in her sly smile that she was not very gung-ho about my arrival. Giving me a telling glance, 'boy, in this part we don't treat guests as gods. So please find some other place to stay as quick as possible.' Behind me, Pinocchio was quarrelling with the cab driver.

'How the hell is your meter reading 220 rupees? Are you a con-artist or something? Which village are you from? This is Bombay, and here we pay only 180 for this far. So take this and get lost.' The driver didn't retaliate, adjusted his groin, took the money and drove off. We walked in.

It was a small house, a room, a small hall and a kitchen. The room was occupied by Pinocchio and Khurshid and the small hall at the entrance was for nose-pecker. A mattress lay on the floor with a ruffled bed sheet, as messy as my condition after the tiring long journey. I was to share the mattress with nose-pecker till I find a place to live in this wild city.

I went inside the lightless bathroom for a quick shower. My eyelids took their time to settle in the darkness as the bulb was not working. Once adjusted, the first thing I spotted was a wall lizard. I missed a heartbeat. The difference between my face and the lizard's face was not much. It was inching closer, step by step towards its prey, a mosquito, ignorant about the death which was now only a few minutes away. I didn't interfere. Why should I? Isn't that the trick to survive in this city? Mind your own business. The lizard with a flick of its tongue had the mosquito. In some odd way, it did make me feel comfortable as well. The mosquito could have sucked on my blood, made me his food, but now, he was no more. Relieved, I took a bath.

In the evening, I stepped out to check the city. I crossed a thousand small vendors on the way to the main road. There were so many cars in Bombay. My belief that there are only Maruti eight-hundreds in this world was squashed. There were sleek cars, long ones, small cars, van types, convertibles, and a very prominent feature on the Bombay roads, red public buses. I noticed some double deckers as well. A bus with a *first floor*. It was quite scary. Full with people on both the floors. When the bus would take a turn at the bend, it would look like a few people in it would spill out. But it goes on the same. Bumping, humping. The people as good as monkeys, know to hang in there well.

I walked a little more and stopped outside the Andheri Railway station. A quaint look of a local train coming to a halt, people getting out in a swarm, getting inside in herds, and the train again on its feet. All in a couple of minutes. Curious and intrigued, I wanted to get a closer look. I went and stood near the ticket counter. Long, never ending queues welcomed me. So long that people themselves didn't know which counter will they end up on. I noticed lines were generally full of men. Women hardly feature in such long queues. They stand near the window, flutter their eyelid, give a flirty smile and ask the man near the window to buy one for them as well. The man wouldn't mind, and the woman's job will be done. It will be quicker, if the woman is a girl, and will be much easier if the girl is in a skirt. 'Woman power!' I wish ammi was here, she could have seen that this part of the world is not only equal, but in fact, positively biased towards women.

While standing near the counters I also noticed a thousand illegal advertisements that covered the walls of the ticket hall.

"Work from home, Earn Millions in Minutes".

"Learn to Repair Mobile Phones. Become Rich. 3000 Rupees course. (Chinese sets included)"

The one which caught my attention was this one.

"Place available in Hostel. Cheap and Comfortable as Hell. Call 9833690224."

I quickly made a note of the number and then entered the station. I stood at the platform transfixed, watching the rowdy and robust crowd. I watched around a dozen trains entering-leaving the station. It all looked so messed up. Hotchpotch. Mish-mashed. A train would enter, the crowds would run with the bogies. People would jump out even before the locomotive stopped. Watching it repeatedly for a dozen times, I was overwhelmed by the energy. Every two minutes a train entered, but the crowds remained the same. Unbelievable!

I was trying to crack a code. Finding and trying to learn the trick by which one can make their journey easier. When someone suddenly blocked my vision. 'Can I see your ticket please?' I thought he was talking to someone else. I looked behind. There was no one other than a cow munching a few poly-bags peacefully. 'Sir, I am not going to take a train. I just want to see these local trains.' The ticket checker gave me a malevolent smile, 'arre wah, I heard an innovative excuse after a long time. Shut up and pay the fine.' I begged, cried, solicited and didn't hesitate in telling him that I was a country man who doesn't know a jack about this place. He didn't believe me. 'Which village are you from? This is Bombay and you have to take a proper ticket or end up paying the fine.' I had to do away with 260 rupees, just because the moron in me wanted to see the trains and the crowds. That checker's family will eat tonight on *my* 260 rupees.

I scurried straight in the direction of Pinocchio's house, a little shaken by the incident. I didn't give a damn for activities going around. Or god knows may be I would end up doing something stupid enough to get myself arrested.

Khurshid was the only one at home, cooking something in the kitchen. 'Aunty, can I make a call?' The cooker whistled. Spoon and the pan made sounds, but Khurshid didn't bother to answer. On a higher pitch this time, 'aunty, can I make a call?' The cooker whistled, spoon and the pan mated again, but no reply. Almost shouting now, 'aunty, Can I......' She came out. '*Baba*, what happened? I am not deaf. God has given me only two ears and two hands. How can I be at two places? This is Bombay. You don't *shout* like this here.'

Why these people stress so much on Bombay. All right you guys are citified, and we are filthy villagers, but when she said that she only had two hands and two ears, she forgot that she got one mouth as well, and all she had to do was to shout back a yes, or a no. Now in my town they at least know this much for sure. May be this is Bombay and people require ears and hands to speak as well. Big city people, you never know.

'We have already informed your father about your arrival and we don't have money to waste so that you....'

'Aunty, I found a telephone number of a hostel where I can stay.' Her lips which were forming words to abuse me suddenly formed a smile. 'Oh, is that the case. You must have told me *naa*. Come, give me the number, I will help you.' She dialed the number and passed on the receiver.

Love, Lust & Lies

I made a note of the address, rent, and other petty details. Once Pinocchio returned, the first thing Khurshid did was to inform him about my hostel. 'Smart kid! Found a place so quick, and that too on his own.' Pinocchio told nose pecker to take me to the address the next day.

The lights were turned off and it was the hour I was scared the most about. Sharing a mattress with the nose pecker. I doubt if his finger stops doing the hard work even when he is asleep. Ugly thoughts crossed my head, what if he rubs some on me. Yuck! No, I can't sleep with him. I remaining politically correct, politely told him to have the whole mattress while I slept on the floor at a good distance from him. I wanted to leave this place ASAP.

Next morning we were standing at the bus stop. Rehan told me that these are BEST buses run by the govt. for the public. After a wait of little over thirty minutes, our bus arrived. The same red bus I had seen the previous day. Similarly like the crowds at the station, all those waiting at the bus stop pounced on the vehicle like a bunch of vultures. Thankfully, we got a seat. I offered nose pecker my window seat as a bribe to answer many questions boiling in my head.

'Where are we going Rehan?' He took the paper from me, 'see, this paper which has an address written on it in your own hand-writing reads, "Hill road, Bandra west." So obviously we are going to Bandra West.' He looked away. He had promised to return the favor of taking me for an all paid movie trip. I reminded him, 'By the way, Rehan, when are you taking me for a movie brother?'

'Movie, ha-ha-ha.' His laughter quite unexpected.

'What was that ha-ha-ha for?' I said, with an expression showing displeasure.

He lost his ha-ha-ha and came to the point, a little irritated, snapped, 'You think I will go for a movie with you.' Poked me his index finger in the chest, 'with you. Dude, I got class. I can't go around with a weirdo like you. Just look at you. You look like a Talibani militant in that beard. Shave it off before it gets you many more mal-treaters like me. You will be joining the hippest college of Bombay. You will look so fucking out of place. Trust me, your life will be much easier without that unwanted weed on your face.' I had a blank expression. I had no idea that it was such a complex thing for him to go for a movie with me if I carried that beard. 'Get that thing off your face and I will probably think of going for a movie with you.' He pulled my beard lightly and finished his sadistic speech in style.

I didn't ask him any other questions. Kept my box shut, fearing more maltreatment. Regretting my decision of giving away the window seat as a bribe. How disgusting is that. You bribe somebody and still your job remains undone. It's exasperating. You feel so dumb.

A few minutes later we got down from the bus and after taking help from a few *paan-walaas* and other small vendors, reached the building mentioned in the address. Let me advise you one more thing here. If you ever get into a situation where you can't locate a building or a particular lane in Bombay, all you need to do is to go to these small *paan* and cigarette vendors. They know their neighboring place inside out. But the best part is, they will help you cheerfully. Their tongues are ever red and their hands ever busy preparing *paans*. I suppose they consider it to be one of their jobs. A responsibility sort of stuff. Make paans, sell cigarettes and navigate people. They will never disappoint you.

We rang the bell to be answered by a bare-chested man in his fifties. Tipsy with a huge-huge potbelly. He was the owner of that place. He took me around the house. There were two rooms

Love, Lust & Lies

and a hall in there. Each room to be shared with a partner. The hall and the first room I checked were already occupied. The plump landlord escorted me to the second room which was probably for me. It was a little bigger than the other room. An extremely thin, anorexic boy was sleeping on the bed in a white pajama and a white vest. He was to be my partner. I looked around, there was a fridge in a corner, an old television set, a small toilet to be shared by all, and a small steel Godrej *almirah*. I was not very keen to live under a roof with five other people, but I didn't have much of an option. Pinocchio and family were no less a trouble. I fixed on this place.

I went back with nose-pecker, picked my baggage, thanked them and fucked off. Khurshid meowed, 'Oh Ameen dear, do visit us whenever you feel like. Remember, this is your home away from home. OK! *Tata*! Take care, *khuda-hafiz*.' I felt like pulling that huge nose ring dangling around her nose. I hope life gives me a chance to do that.

I was back to the building which I was going to call "home" in Bombay. The boy sleeping earlier was awake now, checking out his horoscope in the newspaper.

'Hi, I am Haider.' We exchanged hellos. I settled my clothes in the shelf left empty for me in the almirah, while Haider explained me the ground rules of this paying guest hostel.

'Coming late at night is not a problem, but coming back with female friends is. I don't mind that, but Mr. landlord does. Drinking, smoking, all is allowed, but not in the room. Again, I don't mind that, But.... I guess you know who does. And the most important rule, pay your rent on time, because all that *tharkee* landlord of our room cares for is money. He needs it for his whisky bottles so that he can remain tanked up as always.'

Till here it was all fine. He continued, 'Our landlord shares this room with us. He sleeps in that corner.'

'What!' I had an appalled look. 'Oh yeah, but don't worry. He never disturbs. They say his wife ran away with the kids and since then these liquor bottles are his wife and family. He fucks a liquor bottle, plays with a liquor bottle, and sleeps with a liquor bottle.' I have to share a room with a loony drunkard. The thought was bloodcurdling.

I asked him to introduce me to the guys staying in the other rooms. 'All are dumb-fucks. Don't take the pain. I am living here for the last two years and I know them just by their faces. Nerds and geeks are staying in this house. Man, all these assholes know to do is to read a book or solve some acute mathematical problem. Now how sad is that. They hardly walk out of this dungeon. I mean, you are staying in a city like Bombay. You don't have a girl friend, or you don't screw girls. It means you don't have a *pee-pee* down there. You don't drink, you don't smoke, you don't eat non-veg stuff. It means you don't have a taste. Combine the two and it means that you don't have a life. What the *eff* are you doing here then?' I liked the style in which he censored the four letter 'F' word.

Haider was an anorexic man with hair long enough to cover his cheek bones. To see him speak in that fashion was quite funny initially. But he became so fierce growling all those lines that his words really gripped me. Saliva dropping loose from the side of his lips inadvertently, eyes holding my eyes, words strong and impact-full. His oratory skills were at par with Adolf Hitler.

'Do you read horoscopes in the newspapers?' He asked.

'No. Do you believe in all that?'

'Yes and no.'

'What do you mean by yes and no.'

Love, Lust & Lies

'See, whatever these astrologers write, things happen exactly contrary to that. For example, today it said, *a lonely day ahead. No friends will find time for you.* But see, what happened. You are here. I have a friend, an accomplice. I don't need these rotten bastards. Now *we* will party. Drink like a camel, eat like a pig, swing in different women every night and life will be one grand mad bash. Welcome to Bombay mate.'

I was unable to utter a word. No way he gave me a chance to tell him that I don't drink. It's a sin. I don't smoke. It kills. I don't screw ladies. But I do have a pee-pee down there. Watching the passion and the flare with which this man spoke held me back.

I didn't know then what all this city was going to teach me. What all was I going to learn about it? How many colors of Bombay would be unraveled. What is this city about? But today, I know some secrets about this crazy place. The kind of information I can provide, no book can give you that. You see, these authors who write those fat books, mostly travel in those sleek cars with tinted glasses. But to know Bombay, you have to be on your feet. This is not just a metropolitan city. This city is not just about the tall majestic buildings, sleek cars, discotheques, flyovers, traffic jams, or the glitzy, glamorous world of films. It's much more. Be with me, you will find out *what's* that much more.

The next day of my life was going to be one of the most important ones. It was time to attend college. It was time to meet new people. New *interesting* people. The next pages of my life will tell you how my college kicked off.

Just a word on that. It began with a lot of chaos and flew me into a rage.

One of the major problems of living in a city like Bombay is that it takes at least an hour to go anywhere from anywhere. The distance can be a kilometer or hundred kilometers. Very rarely will you make it in less than an hour's time. The first lecture used to start at seven in the morning. It meant that I had to get up at five, get ready and reach the Bandra station by six, take a jam-packed train, get down at Church-gate station and rush to my college.

Attending college in Bombay is one thing, and *reaching* on time is another. If you have ever taken trains in this city, you will know how difficult it is to catch one going towards South Bombay in the mornings. The moment you see a train approaching, blowing its horn, standing at the platform you need to gird your loins for war. Because all the coaches are bound to be jam packed. No space to breath. Good enough to suffocate you to death. Bombayites every morning don't leave their houses for work alone. They leave for war, and if they survive, they reach their offices.

You will see men in cotton shirts and trousers, top two buttons of the shirt open, chest hair all white, not due to age, but because of an overdose of talcum powder. They will be all around on the station in the mornings. They all are gamblers. Legal gamblers. The biggest stock exchange of our country, 'Bombay Stock Exchange' also happens to be at Church-Gate. So every morning after bribing their gods, they leave to gamble some.

I was sweating profusely the first day I reached college. Courtesy; Local Trains. My shirt drenched, crumpled. Nervous, I already was. As always, things inside my stomach moved. I nosed out tough times lay ahead. I walked in my classroom, lecture already midway. It was an air conditioned room. Wow! I have achieved something, I thought. From attending classes sitting on the ground to tables and chairs to an air conditioned classroom. Not bad! I was making progress.

All around me were uber-cool kids belonging to the ultra rich families. Sons and daughters of heavyweights and big shots of this city, with a surname which means a lot more than just a surname. And in between all of them, was me. Ameen Jalal. Son of a nobody whose name, surname, pet name, all combined doesn't mean anything more. It's just Ameen Jalal. In a way I was proud of this.

But do I really *belong* here? Is this place really for me? Will I settle in? Is it going to be a bumpy one or a smooth one? Questions sprung and my eyes got active scrutinizing the room. Well dressed, sophisticated gentry. Jeans, T-shirts, sneakers, hair gelled, funky mobile phones, bracelets, steel watches. Shaved, all clean. Nobody carrying an iota of hair on their cheeks. My pleated trousers, plastic strap watch, hairdo tousled. And my beard, my everlasting beard. All these made me a bit nervous. Apprehensive.

Where do I fit in this crowd? May be like a square peg in a round hole. Or like a teetotaler around a bunch of whisky gulpers. There were some poor souls like me as well. You can spot them out by their hairstyles. A proper crew cut. Clean and well oiled. That typical nerds parting from the right side. I found solace in them.

After a few lectures I walked down to the canteen. The name was Butterfly café. The place was not very big, but the number of students in there was definitely very big, thus making it look very congested. Full of chirpy young people, talking in English all around. All belonging to my age group. There was *something*, something which was making me feel that I didn't belong to this diaspora. What was that something? Now I had to figure it out. May be it was their fluency in English which was making me nervous. Or my beard and my attire. One of the two, or may be both.

The counter serving Chinese food looked pretty busy. A couple, hand in hand passed me with a plate full of stuff which looked full of fried caterpillars. I overheard the name, 'chow-mein.' It looked weird, sounded weird, but left me intrigued. I repeated the name so that I don't forget, *'chaaoo-meen.'* Soon I had a plate full of caterpillars in my hand. I looked around for a free table and spotted one just behind a gang of girls. I sat down to enjoy my new find.

I have a bad habit of overhearing people. So much so that I end up doing that unintentionally as well. There was one very peculiar and funny thing about the way these girls were conversing behind me. One of them would leak out some information, and the other two would repeat in sync; 'Haw! What are you saying?' Whatever topic, whatever information, the reaction was fixed, 'Haw! What are you saying?' There is a certain tune in which they say this line. An over dramatizing tune. Try and say this line with your eyes big, expressing surprise, 'Haw!(small gap)What are you *saying*?'

Their topic changed to the recent bomb blasts that ripped the city apart. The one sitting just behind me preached, *'uff,* these Muslims. When will they learn? They all have gone mad, exploding every place. I tell you, my heart speeds up whenever I see a man in a Kurta-Pajama and a beard.'

The other two shrieked, 'Haw! What are you saying?'

'And the funniest part is that these dodgy characters keep a beard without a moustache. Now how ugly and scary is that.'

I was no more interested in the caterpillars in my plate. I wanted to quickly get out of this place. Uneasy, I sat there, waiting for these whores to leave. I didn't want them to see me with that beard. A little later they all got up. I moved my eyeballs and registered their faces in my head.

Within minutes I rushed back to the railway station, took a train and was back in my room. I stood in front of the broken mirror fixed on the wall. I checked out myself intently. I took off my shirt. Bare chest. I then took off my trousers. A little later I was nude. I turned, twisted, and inspected myself. Everything was perfect. Everything was very much like these rich Bombay kids. Everything but the beard. I focused on the beard and held it tight. Pulled it, it didn't come out. Pulled it harder, it didn't come out. What did that girl find scary in a beard? It quietly remained where it was. It was not poisonous, not toxic, not injurious, not detrimental, and not destructive.

Why did she say that it is scary then? I didn't have a clue. I got dressed again, still standing in front of the mirror. A little tensed, I tried to scare myself. 'Huaah!' I growled at myself, hands making a claw in the air like those ghosts in C grade movies. 'Huaah,' I tried again, but surprisingly I didn't get scared, my balls didn't freeze. What the hell the world finds scary in a beard.

'*Miyan*, what are you up to?' Haider was standing behind me, watching me growling. I don't know when he sneaked in. Hopefully, he didn't see me naked.

'Why are you grunting like a pig? Is everything all right?'

'Yeah, I am fine. I was just trying to amuse myself.' I had asked him to show me some cheap restaurants around where I can get good non-veg stuff. He was going out for lunch so I joined in.

The roads were busy as usual. Hill road is full of small shops famous for cheap clothes, cheap foot wears and cheap accessories, especially for women. It's a busy road since women kind of lose their rationality when they come to know of a place selling cheap products. They are actually quite cheap. You walk through that road, cross another busy junction and you will end up at Bandra station.

You will notice that I am talking a lot about these railway stations and local trains. But that is sacrosanct. Generally when people talk about Bombay, they end up discussing Hindi films, hero-heroines, share bazaar, sensex, rich night life etc. etc. They don't know about the trains and more importantly the railway stations of Bombay in detail. These tourist guides will take their buses everywhere, right from Hajji Ali to Bhindi bazaar to Amitabh Bacchan's house but not to any railway station. These railway stations are the places where one needs to stand and look at the energy around. I can bet that the energy created by nuclear fusion stands no chance in front of the energy of the crowds present here. People from all walks of life are there. You need to see it. I make an appeal to all the tourists coming to this city to please stand outside one, and check the buzz out. It's mind boggling. I bet, whites will finish their camera rolls over there clicking pictures endlessly.

Another important thing to note is, that whichever station you may get down at, may it be Andheri, Bandra, V.T., Sion. Any one of it. The majority of the population occupying these areas are Muslims. There will be a mosque around. The building of the mosque will be so old that it can fall off any minute, or alternatively it will be getting renovated. For some odd reasons the renovation work in these mosques will never get over.

Obviously, the Muslims living in these areas are very-very poor. All of them down at their heels. Most of them are butchers, pirated CD-DVD sellers, pickpockets, and small restaurant owners. Haider brought me to one such restaurant.

'This is hotel *Yaadgaar*. The food is delicious, cheap rates make it more delicious,' Haider winked. Steaks of chicken and mutton, garnished in thick orange gravy, hanging upside down were some small pieces of tandoor to attract customers. These restaurants are small, but they mean business, and they are excellent managers. Every inch of their ramshackle is effectively used. There will be a table and a chair in every possible free space. Later there may be no space leftover to walk, but it hardly matters.

We took a seat near the refrigerator which had Sachin Tendulkar diving for a bottle of a cola drink on one side, and Shah Rukh Khan on the other. These two names were huge by now. Though I have my doubts if anyone ever bought that cola drink because he/she saw these two diving for one.

Haider called a young boy in his teens, who was walking around in shorts and a body fit T-shirt, with a metal locket around his neck. A *pucca tapori* - a street smart. He asked for the menu card. The waiter boy dropped two paper pamphlets covering all the dishes they serve. It was something like this-:

YAADGAAR MEENU

Chicken Masala -	30
Chicken Korma -	35
Chicken White -	40
Chicken Tikka -	55
Chicken Biryani -	25
Mutton Biryani	15
Plain Rice -	08
Pulao Rice -	10
Rumali Roti -	3.5
Paratha -	05

*all rates above are for half plate!

Haider with his eyes on the menu card, explained me a few things which this menu tries to hide.

'See, mutton biryani is just for 15 rupees. It means that this is beef biryani and not mutton biryani. You know, beef is much cheaper than mutton.' He was more intelligent than I thought.

'Always order the cheapest chicken dish on the menu. Because at the end of the day, no matter which dish you order, it's all the same. They all are cooked in the same gravy. The only difference is in the rates.' He explained further, 'Suppose you call for the forty rupees dish, let's say, "chicken white." Now, in that you will get a bigger piece, but with more oil and color than the thirty rupees dish. It's at your discretion. Either to eat a small piece with less color and oil, or to eat a bigger piece with more color and oil.'

It was all a bit confusing. I told him to order on my behalf as well. Haider ordered two different dishes. The waiter boy made a note in a small diary with a pen which was placed between his skull and the flap of his right ear. He then shouted out our order to the cook on the stove. I kept my gaze on our waiter. These waiters do some disgusting things.

They will hold a glass with all their fingers well dipped inside the glasses and with the same hands serve the customers, wipe the tables, pick dirty plates, pick their nose and hold their thing as well when they go for a pee break. I have my doubts if they ever wash their hands. They are soaked in sweat, customers not minding to eat the sweat fallen in their dishes. It's all like that. You need to go there. Now that's Bombay. Nobody minding nothing. *Sab chalta hai!* Tourists, are you listening. Try having lunch once over here.

Waiting for our food, nothing to do, Haider then asked me, 'Do you like watching films?'

'Oh yeah, I love them.'

'Well, I work as a film editor.' I had no clue whatsoever what does an editor do.

'When the shooting part of the film is done, the tapes come to me. I work on them on a computer, clean it up, refine it and its only once I have completed my job that the film gets ready to be screened.' Interesting. Whenever the word, *'films'* comes up, the glitzy, glamorous picture comes to mind, and leaves a certain amount of fascination.

'Oh wow, you work in the film industry. Great! So you must be meeting these actors, hero-heroines, regularly.'

'Oh yeah, everyday. These big stars, big directors, all come and sit next to me like servants.' They sit like *servants*. My god, I am sitting with a big man.

'Do you get to see shootings and all?'

'I can go on the sets, but I prefer not to. Who is interested in seeing these jokers dance and perform. I am happy in my editing room.' He tried hard to keep a straight face. He didn't know that I am his pop when it comes to lying.

The waiter then served us our two dishes and some chapattis. Haider was absolutely correct. The two had the same gravy. The costly one had a bigger piece, loaded with oil and color, while the cheaper one exactly the opposite.

We were munching our food when his cell phone rang. He took it out in style, opened the flap and placed it on his ear and held it with his right shoulder. He talked and munched at the same time. 'Busy man,' I thought. I was getting more and more impressed. This man works in the film industry, works on a computer, stars sit next to him like servants, and he also carries a cell phone.

A little later he closed the flap of his phone and kept it down. 'Do you know who made these phones. Americans, Chinese, Japanese or Pakistanis?' He asked. I was a little puzzled by his strange question. 'Tell me the person's name and I will cut his balls and feed them to the vultures.'

'Why? What happened? Is your phone not working properly?'

'*Naah!* Not that. Do you have a girlfriend?'

'Well, I do like a girl, but I don't know if she is my girlfriend.'

'Does she tell you to make her a phone call every half an hour?'

'No! In fact, it's been long since I even talked to her.'

'Then you don't have a girlfriend. Or maybe you don't know what a girlfriend is. I have an advice for you. In life, either make a girlfriend, or keep a cell phone. Never ever make the mistake of keeping both these things at the same time. You will go mad. By the way, what's your number?'

'*Unh*, actually I don't have a phone.'

'What the *eff* dude. Every rickshaw driver is having a phone these days. You *need* to carry a phone. Don't eat if required to save for one, but it's imperative.'

'Actually I don't need one. It is of hardly any use?'

'It's not about use. Phone is just not a phone these days. A man without a phone is no less than a paralyzed man.' This was news. I had always believed that cell phones are '*rich people*' products. When did drivers and coolies start buying cell phones? When did this great change happened?

'India is changing rapidly my friend. Cell phones are the latest bug which have bitten us. And quite badly so. What you can do is, use an extra phone that I have at home. In the meanwhile, I will see if I can get a cheap second hand or a Chinese phone for you.'

Waiter brought the bill, Haider didn't give me a chance to even look at it. He paid it. My love grew stronger for him. He left a five rupee coin as well for the waiter as a tip. I had to learn these things. These big city manners, etiquettes. He then went to a small shop, the same cigarette shop where I had asked the address of my building. He bought a pack of cigarette. We sat down outside on our compound wall. Haider took out the cigarette pack and offered me one. I declined. He then placed one between his lips and lit it with a lighter.

'Why do you smoke? It's as good as burning your hard earned money?'

'I smoke because it calms me down. It makes me feel at ease.' I don't know how that is possible, but I didn't care to ask more on that. I had a better question in my head.

'How much do you earn Haider?' I asked. The way he paid my bills, brought a cigarette pack, cell phone and all, left me curious and forced me to ask that question.

'15-30 thousand roughly. It depends though. Depends on the amount of work I get in that particular month. Why?'

'Just like that.'

'Man, anyone can earn in this city. Why is every Tom, Dick and Harry flocking to this city? Any Tom, Dick and Harry can earn over here.'

'Can I earn as well? Is there any kind of part-time job available for me? I don't mind being Tom, Dick or Harry. Either one will work.'

'Of course you can. What are you good at? Is there anything you are specialized in?' Now that was kind of a googly. What am I good at? I am good at lying, but that is not the correct answer to this I suppose.

'I am good at...unh...good at...unh.. good....' Haider made out that I was good for nothing. 'Okay, not a problem, but you can speak English, right.' I nodded slowly. I was not very fluent, but I didn't mention that.

'Great, let me see, I will talk with a friend, he works in a call center. May be you can also work there. Take calls and make calls to the whites and earn a good-fat sum.' He took a long-thinking puff of his cigarette, 'It's not possible that you are not good at *anything*. No sport, studies, or any other activity.' Sport clicked a button in my head.

'Yeah, there is one sport, which I loved all my life. Basketball,' I shouted. 'I can play basketball very well.' Man, it was relieving to find out that I was good at something.

'Wonderful. So you are a basketball player. Cool. Let's see if there is some requirement of a player in any small club. Don't worry, I will find out.' He then took a long puff. Suddenly broke into laughter. I looked at him flummoxed.

'By the way, can I tell you a secret. I can't hold it anymore.' He gave me a lewd smile. 'What were you doing naked in our room today?' He winked.

I narrated everything. Right from the chow-mien, to the girls, to my insane behavior. We laughed and laughed and laughed till we could not manage anymore. We walked back in.

I found a true friend in Haider. He was somebody who would count all the drops in an ocean for you if he considers you a friend. At the same time, he will cover the same lengths and breadths to hurt you if you are in his bad books. But if I ever need to thank somebody more than God, who made my survival in Bombay possible. It has to be Haider. A gem of a person, a jewel of a friend. And one, who finds a faithful friend, finds a treasure.

Love, Lust & Lies

Bernard Meltzer's lines defines our friendship quite well.

"A true friend is someone who thinks that you are a good egg even though he knows that you are slightly cracked."

Without a doubt, I was the cracked egg, of the two.

My mornings on holidays, i.e. days on which college was either closed, or I didn't wish to attend, used to begin with a long walk. Right from my building to the seashore. Walking on the Bandstand promenade alone used to be the most peaceful time in the course of the day. Cool sea breeze, undiluted in the early hours of the morning, before cars and buses start zipping across making it dirty. Those one or two hours were set out by me, only for me. This suburban area, Bandstand, is home to some of the biggest names, big shots of this country. Tall titanic buildings kissing the skyline one after the other. Haider had given me old cell phone of his, which also had a camera, and I would click pictures of these adorable buildings.

Rich old men, panting, gasping for breath holds the majority of the crowd in the mornings, walking up and down the promenade. I knew they were rich, because walking was a rich man's thing in this part. A glance at their sumptuous shoes, shorts and shirts can tell you that they are rich. Apart from that, they sweat a lot. And this sweat, this morning walk sweat, is a proof that all these rich men are debauched. The poor can't afford to sweat it out in morning walks. Their sweat is precious. They sweat it out at work while these rich sit inside their AC cabins, munching fried snacks, drinking English liquor and fucking their sexy secretaries. They try and wash their sins with that sweat of theirs.

On the contrary, if you visit Bandstand in the evenings, it will be full of young people. Or rather I should say, young lovers. Bandstand has a rock beach. You will find all the poor couples who are dying to eat their partners up, kissing and making out in different corners in the dark. Poor I say, because they even don't have enough money to afford a room where they can do those acrobatic moves in privacy. One can see springing and bouncing silhouettes of a boy and a girl by slightest of concentration.

There are many people who are keen to disturb these poor young lovers. There are police constables. Like the ticket checkers, their family also survives on bribe. In exchange of a few hundred bucks they allow them to continue their love making. Then there are bunch of teenagers who sit around these couples whistling lecherously. For them it's like watching a live porn movie, and that too, free of cost.

But the trophy for the most disturbing elements goes to the eunuchs. These eunuchs have a trademark style. They stand in front of these couples shamelessly and demand money by clapping their hands hard. The girl who was busy till then instantly pulls her mouth out of her boyfriend's mouth. This irritates the boyfriend big time. The eunuch claps hard again, indicating that he/she will not leave, until and unless you show him/her the money. The boy will take out his wallet, hand over a few notes, if satisfied, the eunuch will pull the boyfriend's cheek lovingly, blow a kiss and leave. The girl will again go inside her boyfriend's mouth.

When the testosterone runs high, you don't see any distractions, only attractions. May be that is why this place is still a favorite with these sexually desperate and frustrated couples. I calculated quickly in my mind. If I open a room service out here, it will make me a fortune. Shit load of money. I can charge thousand rupees an hour or more for renting out a room to these morons. And because of these infinite govt. run Aids awareness advertisements, which are scarier than those Hitchcock films, they don't want to take any kind of risk. Therefore I can also end up selling a two rupee condom for a hundred rupee. They won't mind paying that sum in emergency.

These days many similar business ideas were coming to my head. The reason being, 'money.' The financial monthly aid that abba was providing me was *just* good enough to cover my expenses. I wanted more. Bombay does this to everybody. It invokes a desire for money. A desire to earn more than you are getting. It teaches you the importance of money. But more than that, it teaches you that with fat money in your wallet, the possibilities are endless.

It was very difficult to get a hike from abba's side. Easier option was to look for a job. I had asked Haider to find one for me. He had told me about a Basketball coach requirement at a small club. I had jumped at the idea. He said that he will let me know in a week's time. Let's see, if basketball does the trick for me once again.

That was also the year of Olympics. Rajyavardhan Singh Rathore was the lone silver medalist from India. All the news channels said that we all are very happy and proud of the feat achieved by Mr. Rathore. Sure we were. But there was something more we were happy about. We were *relieved* that in a country where a billion people reside, there is somebody who saved us the blushes. Saved our ass. But till when will we be satisfied with one silver or two bronze. It's time for more. It's time for these officials who make decisions against these squashed lobbyists, to get up and do something about it. But *when*, is to be seen.

At college I was finding it difficult to strike a conversation with anybody. Always conscious of my beard, my pleated trousers and the shirt. This all used to force me to keep my head low, look around discreetly. My naked session was not good enough to find out what was so weird in me or my attire. Or maybe I was just overtly conscious, living in an illusion that these rich dumbfucks find me weird.

Love, Lust & Lies

To be honest, the way some of these guys dress up was hard to understand. Quite insane actually. There are students showing off their *underwear* strap. Can you believe that? Whole lot of them roam around with their jeans hung way below their waist, revealing their most valuable asset. Their underwear. In white font against a black or a red background of the strap will be written, Calvin Klein, Jockey, Crocodile, Armani, Pepe, etc. According to them it's cool. That's In. Hell No! What can be cool in showing your fucking *chaddi* strap. Now tell me what's weird, a beard on your face, or your underwear poking out of your jeans.

Actually I learnt later. Underwear is not just underwear anymore. *It's more.* They are no more just a piece of clothe worn underneath. It signifies your financial strength. If you wear underwear of any of those brands I just now mentioned, then you are a rich boy. Obviously if you are wearing assorted underwears like Rupa, Samba, you will not show the strap off. Means, you are a poor soul. That's the inside story I am giving you. Quite literally.

At the same time, my English was getting better and better with each passing day. I was learning new words from various sources. There is a place in particular where one can learn a lot of words and enlighten themselves. And that place is the '*toilet.*' You walk in any men's toilet, (ladies toilets, I can't say about) no matter if it's your college toilet, a restaurant toilet, station toilet, or a toilet in a mall. Any public toilet will serve the purpose. Close the door, and right in front of your eyes will be a web of graffiti. The whole door from inside will be scribbled.

There will be a few numbers left for you, invites for threesomes, foursomes, gays and gigolos. There will be a beautifully drawn figure of a nude girl. Trust me, figure wise, that girl will be smoking hot. I learnt all the parts of a woman's body in there. The great artist will take great care and pay close attention to the details. All the complex areas of a woman's body are revealed. The peons or the college administration will never take the pains for cleaning it out. They know it's a place where students are learning hell lot of things.

Who all do so, I thank them. I had never studied Biology and my knowledge about a female body was nil. The great Indian public toilet was the place where I attained such knowledge. Hats off! Really! Sitting on that commode, shitting, it's no joke to make a figure with that attention. Mind blowing!

The Parliament elections were held and as a surprise to many, UPA came to power under Sonia Gandhi. But the real politics began after that. A great political drama. Some people were not happy with Sonia Gandhi taking the prime minister's seat. They said she is an Italian. Silly fools. Look at this Italian carefully. She is deciding many of their fate today. The Indian public didn't notice her nationality when they voted? Why were they cribbing then? Why do some people focus on issues which are not at all significant? Ultimately, Dr. ManMohan Singh replaced Mr. Vajpayee as the new Prime Minister of India.

With a new govt. at the centre, I got a job offer as well. Manmohan Singh was turning out to be lucky for me. Haider gave me the good news. A professional basketball club had called me over for a meeting to be their coach. To decide if I fit the bill or not.

The D-day arrived and I was all set to go for the interview in my pleated trousers and a white shirt.

'Best of luck brother.' Haider was standing at the door with two chocolates in his hands. 'Take this. Have it just before you walk in. Chocolates boost confidence.' He handed over one.

'Thanks man! I will need a lot of that.' I took a deep breath, eyes on the other chocolate still in his hand. 'Very nervous you see.'

'Then keep two.' Haider handed out the second chocolate as well.

With two chocolates in my hand I took an auto rickshaw. Glad that I was able to extract that extra one from Haider. It meant that my smart sense was working and meeting should go fine.

I reached the place, met the lady at the reception. She made a call, talked with somebody and escorted me to a room. I went in. A nerdy old man sat on a revolving chair. He glanced at me from head to toe, with fingers of his right hand constantly tapping his bald head. I stood quietly in front of him.

'Can I see your resume?' I remained quite. All the confidence that I had gained by stealing the chocolate went for a toss. 'Do you have a resume?'

'No sir.'

'Oh, I see. Okay, then have you coached anyone before.'

'No sir.'

'Wow! Interesting. So you must have played *professional* basketball somewhere?'

'No sir.' His fingers stopped tapping his head. He leaned forward on the table. A sly smile now graced the oldie's face.

'And you have come here to coach a professional team.' I was still quite. 'Okay forget all that, have you ever *played* basketball before?' Now that was to humiliate me, but I liked this question more than any of his earlier ones. At least it gave me an opportunity to open my mouth.

'Off course sir. I played all my life at school.' That was good enough for the oldie to make out that it was by accident that I was standing in that room. I was shown the way out. Dejected, I reached the gates of the club.

'Hey you, bearded guy.' A voice exclaimed. I looked up. 'You are Haider's friend, Ameen. Right.' Walking towards me was a dwarf. Or a man little taller than a dwarf. He was in a pair of track pants and sports shoes. He took my hands in his, 'Hi, I am Suresh. Haider told me about you. He said you have a beard, but play basketball very well. That's how I recognized you. Well, I was the one who referred your name for the interview. So are you all set?'

How ridiculous of Haider to use my beard as an identification mark, I thought. I told the dwarf about my meeting with the old nerd.

'Oh man. You have never played any professional basketball before.' He took a deep breath. Picked his nose and then mashing the gold he had excavated and said, 'when Haider told me about you, I presumed that you must be a pro. He said that you need a job badly.' He looked up at the sky, figured out something and then patted my back. I abused him for touching me with those dirty hands of his. 'Never mind. I have another place where you can train people at basketball. Without being a pro.'

My eyes gleamed once again. The dwarf took out his cell phone and made a call. He talked in a language which sounded gibberish to my ears. I waited with a bated breath. Hung up!

'All right! There is a job.' I instantly made a wish, god, give this dwarf a good height next life. 'There is a job of a coach, not for a team, but for the kids of a society in Lokhandwala.'

'What! How can I train some kids? They won't listen to me. I am not some school teacher, but a basketball player, brother. I may not be some pro-shro, but you can't degrade me like that.'

I hope that god was doing anything else but listening to my prayers when I made that wish for the dwarf. He deserves this punishment. Raising hopes and then squashing them.

'Agreed, it's not a team, but where's the harm? You go there. Sit there. Get your money, fuck off.' The dwarf showed me the brighter picture. 'You see, these rich kids of today. They hardly come out to play in the open. There are these new things called computers, videogames and television. These children pee on computers. Shit on videogames and fuck on television. So don't worry.'

Now whatever this dwarf meant by that, I took it up solely because I needed money. He gave me the address and told me to be there sharp at four. I thanked him and left.

Next evening I got ready and left quietly. Unlike yesterday, when I had stepped out with so much excitement and enthusiasm, and with Haider's wishes and chocolates, it all ended up miserably. Thus, I decided to leave without any of these. And guess what? It turned out to be worse.

I reached the building and stood outside, counting the floors of two gigantic towers facing each other. Now when you enter these huge buildings, there are shit load of problems you can come across. The guard at the gate, generally a *Gurkha* who fled from Nepal probably 3-4 decades back in search of work, will question you as if his pop owns those mammoth buildings. But he will only misbehave with you till the time he thinks that you belong to his caste. That is, the caste of servants, coolies, waiters, drivers, gardeners, guards etc. The moment you sternly say that you belong to an upper caste, that is a coach, trainer, tutors, educated middle class caste, he will relax. And if you are from even a higher caste, that is a guest, relative, doctor, boyfriend, he will shit in his pants but not forget to salute you. That is their modus operandi. Gauge your caste, respect you accordingly.

On my first day, the Gurkha was busy with his crime novel. Those thick, cheap Hindi novels with over dramatic endings. Probably the antagonist in his novel had just hunted another victim, raped her, or stole her kidney or had done some bizarre stuff. For this I can say because I could read that in his malevolent smile.

'Who are you, what do you want?' The Gurkha demanded, his smile long gone, brows shrunk.

'I am a basketball coach.' Brows relaxed now, 'oh yeah, boss told me. Go in, cross that lawn and the basketball court is right there.'

I crossed the lawn and my happiness knew no boundaries. I was back on a basketball court. There was a ball lying between the two poles that support the ring. The ball was lying there as if just waiting for me. In a flash my legs picked up speed. As a magnet attracts iron, a basketball attracted me. I grabbed it in my hands, sniffed it, the rubbery fragrance filled my nostrils after quite a long time. I threw it in the ring, then again. Over and over again. So happy I was with the ball, that I almost forgot about the job I was here for. Lay up shots, two pointers, three pointers, I tried them all. I played all alone, not worried, not caring for anything, till my legs gave away. Till every bone in my body refused to budge anymore. My shirt drenched in sweat, I sat down on the ground.

Sitting with my head between my knees, I saw two silhouettes walking towards the court. 'It's time for the job to begin Ameen. Stand up.' I told myself. The silhouettes kept on getting bigger and bigger. A woman and a girl were coming my way. And then it was time for the shocker of shockers.

Right in front of me was a face I would have never liked to see. It was the same girl who was passing comments in the college about Muslims turning terrorists. She had also cribbed that people with a beard less the moustache look ugly, scary and dodgy. The same girl who had ruined my first date with *chow-mein*. I ran my hands to check if my moustache was in place. No! I had just shaved it off. Fuck! I was screwed. It was like someone just now pushed a naked wire up my ass.

'Hi, I am Mrs. Khanna. Are you the new coach for our building?' I nodded, trying to hide my face. Vulnerable.

'Good, this is my daughter, Priyanka. She wants to learn this game.' The whore came forward and I was pretty sure she would either shriek or faint after seeing my dense beard, *less* the moustache. Things in my stomach moved.

'Hi!' She said, standing still. No shrieks. Her mother spoke again, 'Priyanka, can you please fetch that ball?' I was glad she was not standing in my face anymore.

Mrs. Khanna came by my side, 'You see her walk. Look at her closely.' Now what was she trying to do by making that statement. *Look at her closely.* Are these two here to seduce me. To make a front page headline in the newspaper; "Mother-Daughter duo kill a terrorist disguised as a coach." I tell you, women in shorts and tight tees are dodgier than men with beard without a moustache.

'Did you notice anything?' She asked. Yes, I did notice her plump ass and nice fine legs, but this reply would have meant my termination from the job. Better remain quiet Ameen and let her tell what she wants me to notice. 'No madam, I didn't notice anything.'

'Look, look *closely* at her legs.' She came closer to me. I smelt something wrong. Why the fuck is she telling me to look at her daughter's naked legs and continuously drifting towards me. I looked again. Plump ass, nice legs. Nothing else.

'No madam. I didn't notice anything.'

'You probably have weak eyesight. Can't you see my girl is limping.' *Oh mother! My Gawd!* It was relieving to know that it was not the plump ass and nice legs she was trying to show me. Though the news was sad, I felt much better.

'Her right leg is shorter than her left leg. Doctors have advised her to play outdoor sports as that will help her get more control. Just be a little careful with her.'

'Don't worry madam. I will be.' She left. And now I was all alone on the courts with Priyanka. Still a little apprehensive. Old wounds don't fill in that easily you see. She again stood in my face. Long, jet black hair flowing around. Tight little T-shirt and tight little shorts. That was going to be more difficult than I could have ever thought.

'So, where do we start from?' She asked, gripping her hair in one tight fist and tying it all into one clean pony.

'Today, let's just keep it to a warm up session. From tomorrow we will practice some basics.' She didn't make a fuss about it. She walked around the court, did a few exercises and light skipping, before giving in. All the time, my eyes closely followed her. Obviously not from the eyes of a coach alone. Every swing of her luscious body, her face with a few beads of sweat shining under the setting sun, her clean, absolutely clean legs forced me to look at her.

Though initially I was uncomfortable, but because she didn't abuse me or my beard, the day ended on a good note. 'All right then, I will see you tomorrow.' She waived her hand and turned around to leave. I kept looking at her. Suddenly she turned around. I looked away. I thought she caught me staring and will blast me now. *You bearded mullah, you jehadi, you were checking my ass out.*

'By the way, what's your name?' *Uff*, that was a close shave again.

'Ameen.'

I walked out of the gates. The *Gurkha* was still busy with the novel. A girl, whom a few hours ago I would have not liked to see ever in my life, had just entered my life. I even coached her and stared at her lecherously. Life is like that. You can't plan for it. And even if you do, life never cares a fuck for your plans. I wanted to meet her again, hoping she won't return to her old ways of abusing a man with a beard. And also hoping that she wears the same skin-fit t-shirt, with same little shorts.

As Tulsi Das said; "There are three powerful evils: *lust,* anger and greed. And of all the worldly passions, lust is the most intense. All other worldly passions seem to follow in its train.

Only in our first formal meeting, Priyanka had left me somewhat lusting for her.

When it rains in Bombay, it *rains* in Bombay. You sit on any of those black, greased rocks at Versova beach, facing the sea, and you will be able to see all those titanic black clouds entering the city. All set to spat. You will be able to notice that it's raining a few 100 meters away from you. But not on the rock you are sitting. Soon it will be raining at 50 meters away from you. But still not on the rock you are sitting. It will keep coming towards you. You will just sit there, waiting for the rain to take you away with it.

It will get closer, closer, and then the rain drops fall right in front of your feet. And then in a flash you will be all wet. It's like watching some other worldly stuff happening right in front of your eyes. Some state of the art machine.

Rains bring in pleasant weather and relief from the scorching hot sun for Bombayites. But it also brings in chaos, traffic jams, death of local trains, network jams, and over flowing manholes vomiting everything from stinking debris to animal excrements. The situation gets pathetic.

With rains, you always have some fond memories attached. Playing cards and gulping down several glasses of beer one after the other. Getting dirty while playing football on a muddy field. Knocking down cups of hot tea while reading out stories to your loved one. Hugging your lover tight when completely soaked in the middle of a secluded night road. Assorted.

By far, those showers were the most memorable of my life. I was loving them. The reason being, Priyanka. I was now regularly visiting her. Obviously, as a coach. As the dwarf had suggested, there were not many kids who were interested in Basketball. Most of the time it used to be me and her.

Though sometimes these shaved rascals used to show up. But more than basketball, they all used to be interested in the long, smooth legs of the hot babe. When the ball would be with me, no one would charge to dribble it away. But when the ball was with the hot lass, you need to watch the lust and greed in their eyes with which they used to charge at her. A gentle shove, a slight touch, a mere pat was all they cared for. The ball in her hands was just an excuse. Now this used to bug me big time. Having these rascals all around Priyanka used to rob me of my privacy with her. No matter even if that privacy was right under an open sky. I didn't want anyone around. Just me and her, playing basketball.

In order to do away with these rascals, I devised a plan. On days they all would show up, I would order heavy duty warm up exercises. I wouldn't allow them to even sniff Priyanka. Panting, dying, they would swear not to return. Those videogames and computers are having an effect you see. Day in and day out they are busy on their computers and television sets. From where will they get the stamina to run around?

Time to time intervention of these rascals was not the only problem faced by me. Being alone with a sizzling girl whom you fancy discreetly, for about two hours every day, and added to that, she being in a mini-mini short and a tight-tight top, and still not be able to do much, is a horrible situation to be in. It's like telling somebody to take a bath without getting wet. And the rains just used to make things impossible. Not that the floor used to become slippery or something. But my character definitely used to become slippery at times.

The smell of her sweat in the rain, her hemlines always at the crest, dew on her legs, the roundness of her curves looking much tangible and concrete than ever before were things which were attracting me more than a basketball. All drenched, when she used to charge at me. There were many more things other than the ball which grabbed my attention.

At times I used to feel sick of myself. What the fuck am I doing by watching her like that? Aren't you afraid that your eyes will be pierced with a red hot iron rod for doing that on the judgment day? It's a huge sin. Don't do that Ameen. Promise yourself you won't look at her with those libidinous, lewd look in your eyes. 'I promise,' I would say, looking at myself in the mirror and go back more resolute.

She would come in. Take her top off. I would be a human.

She would tie her pony. Still human.

She would take the ball, practice her shots. Still human.

She would start *running* with the ball. The animal in me would open his eyes.

It would start raining. The animal takes over complete charge now. Tells me to screw the rules. Fuck the laws. There is still a lot of time for the judgment day. Enjoy the moment. And that would be enough. I would jump in. Once a hot chick comes in front of you, you forget everything. All your resolutions, all your determination goes back in your ass, for the ass that is in front of your eyes.

One day, suddenly in the middle of a session, she sat down on the ground.

'No more. I don't feel like playing today.' She gasped. I sat down, obviously, a well hundred feet away.

'Why? What happened?'

'Was all night on the net. By the way, do you have an ID on facebook?'

Face-Book. Face-Book. Face-Book. I repeated the words but that was a clear bouncer. What does facebook mean? What is that? How can one *be* on that thing? Hounded by similar such questions, confound, I remained quiet. It could have turned into an embarrassment, giving her all the reasons to believe that I was a dummel-headed fool. My cheeks almost turned red, when suddenly her mother called out, who came as an angel to save me the blushes. She got up, ran a few steps, turned back, 'do add me as a friend. Priyanka Khanna. Bye. See you tomorrow.'

I went back home. Haider was smoking in the room.

'Haider, what's this Face-Book?'

'It's a social networking site.' The expression of confusion still denying to leave my face. 'Internet. One of the greatest discoveries of mankind. The whole world is there.' Yeah right! This loafer sitting in front of you doesn't know a jack about it, and you say that the whole world is there.

'How can I be on a facebook?'

'Go to a cyber café. Ask the person out there and he will help you out.' Haider made out that it was of no use explaining it to me.

I changed and visited a café. And for the first time in my life I sat in front of a computer. I have no words to describe the sensation of that moment. When you have a computer around you, it's a complete different feeling. A different world. It's a blessing to have one in your vicinity.

It's a box. A magic box. Like a magician takes out a dozen things from his hat, this box also contains a billion things. There is a whole world captured within. A world of knowledge. I became an instant fan. I realized why these kids of today are ditching basketball and other sports for this thing. Nobody can resist the charm of one.

I call it the 'Tic-Tic machine.' You know the sound that comes out when your fingers start doing a tap dance on the key board. Now, in this part of the country, you need to know to use a computer. It's sacrosanct. This Tic-Tic machine is also the place where facebook is. I called the boy at the desk for help.

'Brother, where is facebook on this?' One question was enough for him to sniff out that I was a computer illiterate. He placed his hands on the mouse and the cursor moved. I watched closely. Mugging it all up. A page came up and he stopped. 'Put your ID and password.'

'And where will I get an ID and password?' He burst out laughing. A gas of food waft from his mouth forced me to turn my face away. He then clicked again and opened up a page having a form and told me to fill in my details.

Now I need to tell you about these boys who sit in these cafes. They are not the owners, but mere employees who look after the place. They are no Bill Gates. Most of them are illiterates, or drop outs. Hardly any of them know English. But they still know how to use a computer. When I met this boy, I felt literate and illiterate at the same time.

I know English. They don't know English. They know how to use computers. I know how to *spell*, 'computers.'

He showed off his skills. 'See, when it hangs, click here, restart this way. This is Yahoo, the big red Y indicates that, this is where you click to make an ID. This is where you print from.'

They know enough to serve their purpose. And that's good enough. Nobody can know everything about this magic box. There are shit load of things. These boys are street smart. They look like any of those shoddy characters you see on a local train, but they have great brains up there. Uneducated, yet more knowledgeable than you. Looking at them you have to agree with Cicero when he said; *'Natural ability without education has more often attained glory and virtue than education without natural ability.'*

My form was filled, ID done, and now I was a member of facebook.

'Won't you show me the photograph of your girl?' He said to me coyly yet shamelessly.

'How the hell do you know it's something to do with a girl?'

'Why else people use facebook? It's all about checking out girls. What is the girl's name?'

'Priyanka Khanna.' A clean smirk adorned his face.

Now this has been an old problem of mankind. We discover something great, and then start using it for ulterior motives. Raping and disgracing our own achievements. Like we discovered the nuclear bomb, and now are busy saving them from hoodlums and gorillas who threaten to steal it and destroy the world. Similarly we have started misusing these tic-tic machines and the social networking sites on them. Every other day it's in the news, two strangers befriended each other on the net, met, and 'he' raped 'her.' Or, he kidnapped his friend, killed him later.

My page popped up. The café boy's fingers typed Priyanka's name in the search box. His eyes gleaming nastily.

A progress bar appeared and when the two ends in there met, Priyanka's picture was right in front of my eyes. Making a pout, throwing a kiss at me, with her teddy bear in her lap. *Lucky fat bastard,* I thought.

'How can I add her?'

'Ow, taking bold steps friend. After all, great lust and great love, both involve great risks. Right, friend.' I ignored his comments. 'But what is it in your case? Love. Or lust.' He added her in my list. 'Wow, she is a sizzler. Where do you find such hot bombs.' The boy remarked, his eyes raping Priyanka's picture.

'None of your business.' He broke into a guffaw. I wanted to break his mouth. I paid and left. Happy to learn something about the tic-tic machine and glad to be friends with Priyanka on this crazy thing called Face-book.

That year America was voting. When America votes, the whole world watches. That shows their power. No American needs to know who is India's president, but almost every Indian knows who is America's president. The battle this time was between George Bush and John Kerry. Most of us wanted to get rid of this loony Bush, but America voted for him again. John Kerry, nominee of the Democratic Party was defeated by 34 electoral votes. President George W. Bush was still the president of the United States.

'This lunatic Bush is from Texas. A cowboy.' Haider was drunk that night. He was one of them who had hoped that this election will bring the curtains down to Bush's nuisances. He had mixed whisky and rum in one glass to mourn the victory of Bush. He coined a portmanteau for his drink, and called it "rummisky," Rum plus whisky.

He took a sip and continued, 'do you know how these cowboys hunt?' I shook my head. 'They sit on a horse, and with a long stiff piece of rope with a sliding noose at one end in their hands, which they call a lasso, fling it around any animal or cattle's neck.' Innovative people, I thought. 'This Bush is going to do the same. He and his lasso are going to grip the whole world and gag us all to death. Americans have lost it. It's a bad-bad news brother.' He was very sad. So much was he drunk that he kept on jumping from one topic to another randomly.

'You know I lost my father at a very young age. But to be honest, I feel that *everyone* must lose their fathers at a young age. It teaches you to be independent and responsible quickly.' He had lost it. The alcohol was doing its trick. It was funny to hear words like responsibility from a drunken man's mouth. All sloshed.

'You know people like me, people who don't have an old man worth a damn, are to lead a life like this only. Seeking foolish destiny. We remain desperate all our lives running around, and

Love, Lust & Lies

people start feeling that we are lunatics, fools.' He got a bit emotional with that. Fresh bubbles of tears could be seen in his eyes.

'Oh man, this Bush victory made me so sad, look what all I am talking about. Let's change the topic. Let me ask you something.'

He took another sip, 'Have you ever slept with a girl?' The alcohol was now in all the corners of his body probably. I gave him a shy smile.

'You haven't!' His sozzled eyes big in surprise. 'I can't believe it.' A hapless look now, 'Dude, virginity is no dignity, simply lack of opportunity. Do away with it.'

And then he got all charged up. Took a huge gulp, finishing all what was there in his glass. Wore his shirt and said, 'come with me, you are going to make your debut tonight.' Oh fuck, this man has gone crazy, I thought.

'No Haider. Let it be. I am fine a virgin. I love it.'

'Shut up and get up.' He pulled me out with him, started his bike, and soon we were on the roads of Bombay. Lonely roads. Bombay looks so different late in the night. He zipped around and stopped on the Linking road. We noticed two girls standing at a distance. It was almost three in the night. Nobody around. Even the dogs were asleep by then.

'Look there, at that turn stands our *maal*. Our hunt for the night.' My heart started pounding like crazy. He parked the bike and we started walking towards them.

'Haider, let's go back home.' I pleaded.

'Don't worry. I will hump her first and then it will be your turn. Watch and learn while I will be doing it.' *Watch and learn*. Huh! Really, rum and whisky together are very risky. Remember that.

We were now only a few meters away. Honestly, it was quite scary. The two girls noticed us. Moved towards us. I held Haider's hand. He gave me a disgusting look and unstrapped his hand. And then, in that dark moonless night, under the orange glow of the streetlights, I saw a girl only in a bra for the first time. It looked like I would pass off. These girls were as bizarrely dressed as one can imagine. Cheap tight shorts, loud lipstick, big round colorful earrings, and super big, pumped up breasts, as if the whole silicon valley was living in them. Haider looked at me, chewed his lips lewdly, winked, and went to have a word.

He walked confidently, and then his pace reduced. Suddenly, out of the blue, he took a sharp round-about turn. In fact, he came running back to me. As if the girls were some monsters in disguise.

'What happened?' I asked. He kicked start his bike and told me to hop on quick. When he explained me later, I laughed like anything.

'They were not girls.'

'What do you mean by that?'

'I mean, they were not girls, but boys, or what you call a girl trapped in a boy's body.'

'Oh my god. They were eunuchs.' He nodded. His eyes cumbersome still in amazement.

'But who sleeps with these eunuchs?' I asked the curious question.

'People who can't afford girls. Their prices are higher compared to these eunuchs. And also people who like the back door more than the front.' He winked. 'What do you like, front door or the back door?'

'Well, after that night, I would say I prefer the window.' After all, everything that shines is not gold. True! Very true!

I fell ill and was not able to visit Priyanka for a week or so. All my hopes of telling her that I was also on facebook faded away with time. It was still going to take two days to recover completely. I decided to check if she had messaged me back or not. I visited the café again.

The café boy's face broke into a malevolent smile when he spotted me. He whispered in the ear of the person sitting next to him. But that whisper was just pretence. He wanted me to hear that.

'Here comes Mullah-*mastana*. Love-Crazy Mullah. A terrorist who prefers roses over guns.' I didn't react. My head was already occupied with Priyanka. I took a seat and opened my account. I looked around everywhere, no messages were found. I then checked on my wall for any posts. Thankfully there were not one but two. Both, by Priyanka.

The first one read; *Hey Ameen, gud 2 c u on facebuk. But dere is sumthn I discovered which surprised me. V r in d same college. Must meet sumtym. Wil tlk more abt dis in the evening.*

The second one posted two days later read; *where have u been? Not turning up. R u all right?*

My first reaction was, 'Horrible spellings. Madrasa kids will spell better than that. Huh!' The second message was quite difficult to interpret, especially the last line. "R U all right?" Now in which tone was that asked. Was she asking me this as a friend, enquiring about my health. Or asking like a master asks an employee the reason for his absence. I dug out all the reasons which said that it was asked as a friend. Still I convinced myself that she asked this as an employer. I logged out, a little muddled.

I reached the reception to pay the amount to the café boy when he did it again.

He whispered, 'Mullah-*mastana.*' Now this was sheer wrong timing. I was already going nuts trying to interpret Priyanka's message. I was not in the mood to take any crap. I held him by his collars instantly.

'Listen carefully. The next time you say that, I will place a bomb right under your mamma's fat ass. You know, terrorists are good at that. Then with the remote to the bomb in my left hand, I will tell you to strip down. Then this leather belt which is running around my trousers will be in my right hand. And I will change that white ass of yours to pink and then to red. If satisfied, your mom will be spared, if not, she will meet the same fate. Is that understood.' The boy was too nervous to speak up. A bearded man, right in his face, threatening, was too much to scare the shit out of him. I left his collar and moved out. Content. That was the first incidence which made me believe that it's good to be bad sometimes.

Outside, an auto rickshaw cruised by. A boy and a girl were busy inside the rickshaw. Too busy even to notice that the driver was looking in the mirror or the rickshaw standing at a red light and people on the roads witness their doings. In fact, after Bandstand, this is the second most favorite place of these lovers. From now on, please don't blame a rickshaw driver the next time you read a newspaper flash; "Taxi driver rapes a college student." (Can be a tourist sometimes. You know, white skin is a rare opportunity for them. They *seize* it with both hands.)

What else do you expect them to do? Sitting on a running engine all day long, their asses are burning hot, and when these students do some crazy stuff right behind them, oblivious to the fact that he is watching, every part of the driver's body hots up.

But I myself was thinking somewhat on the same lines.

'Will I and Priyanka ever sit in that rickshaw together?'

'Will I ever be able to hump Priyanka in there?'

'Will I be......' Wake up bozo. Look at her and look at you. Carefully. Even her teddy is much nicely dressed than you. And don't forget, you are just an 8000 rupee a month employee. Don't end up doing something stupid. Be patient. Wait! Wait as a night sky waits for a fortnight to see the full moon. Wait as a tree waits in spring for its leaves to return. Wait! And if it's written to happen. It *will* happen.

But Will Rogers says;

"Even if you are on the right track, you will get run over if you just sit there and wait."

So, shall I sit there, or make a move.

"Make a move dearie, it will help."

A year was about to complete in Bombay. But nothing more was happening on Priyanka front. By more I mean, nothing more apart from small chit chats, and exchanging some messages on face book. We used to meet quite often now though. Once in the morning, at college, and then in the evening. Yes, we were friends. But what now. I wanted more. And at such times, times when nothing works for you, times when no ideas cross your mind, this whole city kind of starts gripping you by its pace. The whole city starts teasing you for being stuck. Seems like everyone is showing their teeth and then their bums. They warn you to get your act together quickly or the results can be fatal.

At such times, sitting at bandstand, watching the world past by, I used to feel so alone. It feels like the weight of the whole world is on your shoulders. Everyone is riding on it. My condition was somewhat like the sea. Anxious, eager, nervous and restless. I am pretty sure that these oceans also liked somebody, but their fancies remained fancies. Their love remained incomplete.

Bombay is such a big city. You feel so small, so meek, and timid at times. Fear of losing it all, losing yourself, losing the one you love, your fancy takes over. It makes you feel so vulnerable.

They say noble deeds and hot baths are the best cures for depression. But this doesn't works for me. The best place for me to visit at such times was the railway station. My stress-buster was here. On the roads, in the company of these small vendors and their small shops. Sitting all day long between those rich jerks, I felt so poor and destitute, but at the station I feel rich, because there are bigger beggars all around. The smell of my cheap 50 rupees deodorant suddenly smells intoxicating in front of these people who all smell of sweat and sweat alone. I would sit with these bootleggers, small vendors, and waiters. Just sit with them, and smell them. And I would be relieved.

But it all became a little worse with this news. A series of coordinated suicide bomb attack ripped apart London's public transport system that year. The bombings were carried out by four British Muslim men who were motivated by Britain's involvement in the Iraq War. The bombings killed 52 people, injured 700 others. The series of explosions constituted the largest and deadliest terrorist attack on London's transit system in history.

This news filled me with scary thoughts. Priyanka's callousness towards bearded men will be re-instigated. What if she tells me to bug off? What if she tells me that she no more wants to talk to me? What if she raises suspicion that I am also one of those *jihadis* out here on a mission?

That day at college I tried to keep myself away from her. Making sure that I don't bump into her even by a mistake. But as luck had planned, I didn't bump into her, she bumped into me.

'Hi! Where were you? I looked everywhere.'

'Ah! I was in the library.' Now these Bombay kids don't greet you by waving their hands or shaking hands with you. They come and hug you straight. She did the same. I was still not accustomed to such things. Even though it was a light hug, as friends do, but a hot girl hugging a bearded boy in public is bound to raise a lot of eyebrows. The small one second in which our bodies united, I felt her chest expanding against mine. Quite scary and erotic at the same time.

'Can we go for a smoke outside?' Now that was a shocker.

'You smoke!' I said instantaneously.

'Yes! Big deal.' She said with a straight face.

'No, it's just that, you never told me.'

'I am telling you now. Come.'

We walked out together. That was the first time she was giving me so much attention. Nervousness gripped me. We crossed the road to reach the small cigarette shop surrounded by many shaved rascals. She demanded a pack of Marlboro lights from the vendor. Then took out a fluorescent pink lighter from her bag and did the needful. A small puff and a gush of smoke came out of her mouth.

'I never told you because I didn't know you well then. Now I know you. You will not tell my mother about this.'

'Of course I will not.' I was glad she thinks she knows me well. And very relieved that she doesn't know about the bomb blasts. No more nervous, I advised her, 'girls should not smoke. It's harmful.'

'And boys are allowed to smoke. Isn't it harmful for boys as well, Ameen? Why this discrimination?' She caught the prejudiced part in me. Bad advice. I looked away and thought it's better to change the topic.

'So how was your day? How were the lectures?'

'The lectures went fine, but I got to know bad news. A Parsi friend of mine lost her dad. Do you know what Parsis do with the bodies of the dead?' I don't know why she asked this. I simply shook my head.

'They take it up on a tower, which they call the tower of silence and feed it to the vultures.' With that she took the last puff and squashed the butt of the cigarette. I kept quite. No advise, nothing.

'All right then, I will see you in the evening.' I wanted to leave before she starts telling me other various ways of dealing with the dead bodies. I turned and walked a few steps when she called out.

'Ameen, you didn't ask me how he died?' Why would I want to know that? Why she wants to tell me that? I turned around.

'He died in London.' I missed a heartbeat. 'You know four Muslim men blew four bombs. Four, Muslim, bearded fellows.' I stood there quietly. Looking down at the squashed butt near her shoes. 'Why are Muslims blowing every other part of the world Ameen? What is it with them?'

I opened my mouth, searching for an answer. Failed, and closed it. Again opened, closed. Opened, closed. There was no way I could explain that to her. She waited for a reply and then left.

Those lines from Priyanka's mouth should have disgusted me. Instead, they filled me with rage. Why the fuck should *every* Muslim be looked down upon and walk in the market with downcast eyes if a few dickheads are committing heinous crimes? Why do Muslims need to prove their loyalty for their country again and again? Are Naxals who blow up a police station or a military camp every other day in some part of the country Muslims? Are these groups promoting terror in north eastern part of our country Muslims?

There have been some great Muslim poets, great scientists, philosophers and mystics. But the whole world today knows them for fundamentalism, intolerance and fanaticism. It's a very old community, who is being defamed because of some morons, who are doing nothing but bringing bad name.

Most of the early scientists, physicians, chemists, economists, neurologists, engineers in the world were Muslims. Especially during the "dark ages of Europe." It is some Alhacen, an 11th century Iraqi scientist who is considered the father of optics, pioneer of scientific method and experimental physics. In fact, he is considered to be the *"first scientist"* on this planet.

It is some Jabir Ibn Hayyan who is called the father of chemistry. Some Musa Al Khwarizmi who is called the father of algebra and algorithms. Some Al-Jazari, a 13th century civil engineer, considered the father of robotics and also the father of modern engineering. And the list goes on and on.

Now why the hell was I looking for answers to an annoyed Priyanka's stormy questions. I don't need to. *Balls!*

A few more shaved rascals were buying cigarettes from the same shop. I remember Haider telling me, 'I smoke because it calms me down. It makes me feel at ease.'

I moved towards the shop. Pushed aside a shaved rascal and said, 'One Marlboro lights!'

Every decision is liberating, even if it leads to disaster. Otherwise, why do so many people walk upright and with open eyes into their misfortune?

My decision to start smoking also made me feel liberated that afternoon.

By now I was a big fan of those caterpillars. I loved eating them with a tinge of schezwan sauce. I made it a point to eat it once every week. Schezwan chicken chow-mien. There was one thing though very interesting to notice at shops serving Chinese cuisine. Somehow in every place, you will notice that the person cooking Chinese food will also look like a Chinese man. In all my days in Bombay, I was not able to spot even one person looking like me, Haider, or like the person cooking those *kebabs,* or like these waiters. You will always and always find a slant eyed chap playing with noodles in his pan, flipping it several times, banging the long-big ladle against the pan, like a joker performing in front of an audience.

See, like those Gurkhas are famous for their courage and most of them cross Indo-Nepal border and end up becoming a guard. These slant eyed chaps are famous for their noodles and you will see that most of them end up cooking Chinese at hotels in Bombay.

After all, you do what you are good at. Like me. I was good at basketball and right now I am coach to a beautiful, sizzling hot girl. In fact, the hottest girl of my college. I know she is the hottest one around because not only boys hang their tongues loose when she enters the class, but even the insecure girls do the same. Most of the time she used to sit with her gang of girls. The same gang which was abusing bearded fellows on my first day in college. Hardly I used to see her talking with a boy or sitting with one. Rising doubts in my head of she being a lesbian.

That day outside our college, a guy was mercilessly bashed by two other guys. He was kicked and thumped and punched and boxed. And was left half dead with a sore eye. By the time I reached the spot, the show was over. I enquired from a person who was able to catch the show from the best seat in the house.

He adjusted his groin and with a twig popping out of his mouth said, 'same old stuff. This Romeo went for a movie with his Juliet, but it turned out to be a triangular love story. So the villain came here with his friends and bashed Romeo black and blue. Warned him not to see Juliet again.' He adjusted his groin once again and left. He sounded like he was used to such fights. I decided to find out if Priyanka was having a boyfriend or not. Because if she has, then I had to be careful and let my fantasies be fantasies. Or else one day I can very much end up in this Romeo's shoes. I got an opportunity to ask that evening.

Priyanka's game was showing improvement by leaps and bounds and so was my interest in her. And because I was also a smoker now, we both after every round of play, used to walk into a ramshackle cum cigarette shop, right opposite to her building, and in a dark corner inside the ramshackle would end up a stick. Inside in the dark, so that her rich dad and her over sensitive mom won't catch us.

That day some shaved rascals emerged from the building to watch us play. Or rather I should say, watch *her* play. They stood around the court, with hands on each other's shoulders, watching lecherously. In between one of them would pass an expert's comments and the rest would give a horselaugh. Priyanka never liked them. In fact, at times she used to get too close to me while dribbling the ball when these jerks would be around. Just to make them jealous. My heart would start pounding when her face used to be almost in my face. Pounding nervously and excitedly. Too close for comfort.

Now this time when these assholes came on the courts, their commentator said something really nasty.

"And here goes the girl, charges at the mullah, oh, the mullah has been fooled, and the "Limping Beauty" scores an excellent basket.

That was it! "Limping Beauty" were the words which outraged her. Her ears turned red hot. Livid, incensed, she grabbed the ball again. And as usual started sticking close to me. But today the closeness was too much. Plus there were added ingredients in her act. She was almost flirting with me. Giving me a smile, running her fingers in my beard, with her gaze all the time fixed on the shaved rascals. Her breasts almost rubbed against my chest. To an extent it all did work. One had to see the faces of those rascals. Greedy, lustful, jealous eyes. All wanted to be in my place. All wanted to be *me*. An 8000 rupee a month employee. A mere coach. I gave a discreet laugh. Ha!

In those fearful yet erotic moments, I made a mistake. I stepped on her right foot and she fell down with a thud.

The shaved rascals tittered, hooted like a wolf and left. I ran and sat next to Priyanka. Held her foot and twisted it lightly. She felt better. Actually I ingeniously saw an opportunity in that accident. Those legs, oh god, those legs, whom I was worshipping with my eyes since so long. I was getting an opportunity to touch them. To run my hands over and around them. I just couldn't have let that opportunity run away.

I think we Indians have a thing for legs. I mean, not only sexually. See, a son touches the feet of his parents before getting married, a student touches the feet of his teachers before an exam, and we all touch the feet of those dummy-gods at temples. So it's very obvious that we will love those feet when we get in the bed as well.

I stood up and gave her my hand for support. She gave hers in mine. The whole act was a little too much for her. We decided to take a smoke break and walked into that ramshackle.

Now smoking in that dark room, with a smoking hot girl whose smoking hot legs I had just laid my hands on had left me horny than ever before. I could have worked on myself, but held back somehow.

'Is it my fault that I was born like this. With a shorter leg. But these bastards....' I was glad she hates them. I hate them too. Our thinking matches, I thought.

'Have you ever tried cigarette and tea together?' I didn't like this question of hers. I wanted her to continue abusing those guys. And by no means was I interested in tea, coffee, pina-colada or anything.

'No, I haven't.' She then ordered two cups of tea for both of us. An urchin delivered it within minutes. She took a long drag and then a sip, making a *"shhooup"* sound.

'Ah! This is what you call smoking. This is what you call as freedom. I swear, my parents keep me in a cage. I feel so nice here. In this dark ramshackle.' *What a fucking joke,* I thought. Your parents allow you to wear such clothes, allow you to play basketball, give you a sleek car in which you go around anywhere, and you say they keep *you* in a cage. Come with me to my town and I will tell you what it is to be in a cage.

'The deadly combination of nicotine and caffeine together kills you slowly.' She was yet not over with her scary speech on tea and cigarettes. 'As slow as your blood travels that translucent pipe when you donate blood. It falls down into that transparent pouch. Tup-Tup-Tup. That slow.'

The moment she got over with her speech, I asked her the question, 'by the way, do you have a boyfriend?' *"Shhooup"* She took another sip.

Love, Lust & Lies

'Why do you want to know that?' This girl was turning out to be extremely unpredictable. The way she asked that question, looked like she was again flirting.

'Just like that. Never saw you with anyone at college.'

'I had one. Broke up a few months back.' And my! I could have ended up shouting in exult, but pinched myself and told to control my hormones and senses.

We walked out of the ramshackle. The evening looked beautiful than ever before till she said this,

'You don't need to come tomorrow evening. I am going for a movie. *English* movie.' She said as if I didn't know English. I wanted to ask her if I can join in. But that stress on English, stopped me. And after all, as Pinocchio had said, "who would like to go for a movie with me? I look like a weirdo. Like a Talibani militant." My beard and attire will be a little too much for her and her gang of girls you see.

I had taken another decision. Well. Almost!

From her building I went straight to the mosque. The evening prayers had just ended and the Imam was sitting alone in the lobby reciting the holy Quran.

'*Assalam-Valaikum imam Sahib.*'

'*Walaikum-Assalam!* How can I help you son?' I moved my eye balls to make sure nobody was listening. It was a quiet and a dim hall.

'Imam *sahib*, is it allowed for a man to shave his beard for a couple of days?' He gave me a blank stare. 'I mean, I will get it back soon.' A thin smile graced his peaceful face.

'Well, why for a couple of days. You are allowed to shave it forever. Keeping a beard is not compulsory. It's considered good, holy. It's a sunnat, but not necessary. Allah will be happy to see that on your face, but neither will be angry if it's not there.'

And that was enough for me. I went to a shop, bought razor and a blade and rushed to my home. Soon I was standing in front of the mirror. Looking at my beard. Then a little later looking at my face now covered fully under a thick layer of white foam. The bulb flicking over my head, razor in my hand, heart thumping fast in my chest. Giving it a last thought.

Should I. Should I not. Should I. Should I not. Should I. Should I not.

Yes I should! And the razor flicked. And that was it.

In minutes, I was clean. All shaved. All clear. I was a shaved rascal myself now. It was looking like a completely different Ameen in the mirror. A stranger. I had never seen my face like that ever in my life earlier. Nor had imagined. I introduced myself to myself.

'Hi! I am Ameen Jalal. *Part II.*'

I looked at myself in the mirror for some more time. And then excitement made way for nervousness. It started gripping me. I was no more what I was. As if I just now lost my identity. As if I lost myself. Before that pathetic guilty feeling could seep in, I moved away. I ran my hands around my smooth cheeks. And thought about Priyanka doing the same. It was then for the first time that I liked it. I don't mind being a shaved rascal if it gets me closer to her.

Haider returned a few hours later, late at night, heavily drunk.

'Am I dreaming.' All sloshed, he asked. 'Have you really...shaved....' He came forward, touched my cheeks, eyes became big, gaped and then he fainted.

Next day I got up early and got ready for college. When I went to comb my hair and looked at myself again in the mirror, I felt like my pleated trousers and shirt were not going down well with my new look. I took them off. I opened Haider's almirah. Dug in, and took out a pair of jeans and a T-shirt. I wore them. I went back to the mirror. And guess what? I thought I was the sexiest man god ever made. I winked at myself.

When I reached the station it looked like a similar day when I had ran to watch a movie with Zareen. All eyes pestering me. Asking me, 'Where is your beard Ameen? You shaved it for her. *For her?* You think she will be impressed. Ha! You Dumbfuck!' And then they all showed me their teeth and then their bums.

I reached college, the number of teeth and bums increased. Things in my stomach moved. It was a wrong decision Ameen. It was a *fucking* wrong decision. I sat in the room, quietly. Hiding my face now. Till Priyanka entered. Her jaw dropped open and she smiled.

Then for the first time in my life, for the first time in my entire *fucked up* life, a girl sat right next to me.

'What the hell? You shaved it.' I smiled coyly. 'Well, well, well, you made the right decision. Look at you. You are looking like a different man altogether.' Our thinking matches so much, I thought again.

'Oh mother..., you are wearing jeans. And T-shirt as well. Where did you get them from?'

'I bought them.'

Her eyes checking me still, 'Nice. Very nice.'

That whole day she was with me. Her gang of girls, well who was interested in them. Neither me, and I guess, nor was she. But the cherry on the cake came later.

'Ameen, would you like to come for a movie with us?' I can't tell you how I felt. I again had to pinch myself, real *hard* this time, to keep my emotions under wraps. After all Pinocchio was correct. I removed my beard, and in flew a movie offer.

'For sure I will,' I said in confirmation.

Now the movie going experience was completely different than what I had conceived it to be. In Bombay they watch movies in a multiplex and rarely in a "stand alone cinema hall." They watch quietly and keep popping pop-corns. Now why the hell they keep gorging on so much of pop-corns is still hard to understand. They watch a movie, munch pop-corns, grow a belly and then run on the treadmill to get that belly off. It's like a cycle. Watch, munch, run! Watch, munch, run!

I must tell you, that there is a lot of difference between a cinema hall and a multiplex. The seats over here are better, the air conditioning is better, the sound quality is better, the crowd is sophisticated, but still, in the end, you don't feel like you just now watched a movie. At least, I didn't. You know why? Because nobody *whistles* in a multiplex. It's no fun. It's like sitting in some corporate meeting watching the company's audio visual. It's all so much cultured, so much chic. So much *complex*.

Come to *my* town and catch a movie. Over there, when Salman Khan or the good guy punches the bad guy, the whole crowd punches their fists in the air with him. When the hero-heroine sing a song and dance around the trees, the whole hall dances with them. You are so much a part of the movie. Completely engrossed. Now that is what I call as a movie going experience. That's fun. This was no fun. They all watch it so seriously here. As if they are going to be asked questions the next day. Huh!

It was good to see an English movie though. My belief changed that English movies are all about sex and actresses dropping their clothes like leaves falling from a tree during autumn. The action stuff is great and it's a visual delight. But I felt sad for their stars. They are doing a great job, yet they don't know what stardom is. I mean, living in countries like America and

Love, Lust & Lies

England they are thinking that they are the biggest stars on this planet, oblivious to the fact that their Indian counterparts are bigger. *Check them out guys.* Indian superstars truly define the words star-power. The kind of influence and impact our *desi* stars have, American stars can't even *imagine* that. Not even in their fucking best dreams.

Has Tom Cruise ever influenced anyone's name? Do fans in America keep fasts or performed *havans* when a Marlon Brando or a Clarke Gable fell ill and are hospitalized. Do American taxi drivers prop up the interiors of their taxis with posters of Julia Roberts or Sharon Stone. No they don't. In India, they do. Let me explain myself a bit.

You get down near any railway station in Bombay and walk into these small *udipi* or Muslim restaurants around. And observe the head waiter, who will usually be an obese and the most ugly looking guy calling out the young little urchins serving around. He will shout, "Shah- Rukh, wipe table 6." Or, "Salman, kebabs at table 2."

If the kid is well built, he will be Salman, if he has floppy hair he will be Shah Rukh. They have long forgotten their real names. It all starts like a pseudonym, but eventually becomes their real name. When they run away from their villages or are forced to earn money by their parents, they come to this city with a lot of dreams. Till the time their dream looks realistic to them, their real name exists, but sooner or later they realize that they are going to be servants all their lives. They are given a new name by their new bosses. And then that name sticks with them all their lives. Their dreams are shattered. This city is known as "city of dreams." But to be honest, more dreams have been broken here than fulfilled. It may sound blunt, but a realistic sobriquet for this city will be, *"city of broken dreams."*

I thought that these names are religiously biased as most of the chaps around are Shah-Rukh and Salman. The last time I visited a hotel, the kid who served me tea was a Hrithik. A lot of Aamirs and Sanjay Dutts are also around. *Now that's star power.*

Alternatively, when an Amitabh Bachchan falls ill and is hospitalized, there will always be a swarm of crazy fans who will sit around the hospital, and conclude *havans, yagyas* and many "other worldly" stuffs for the star's quick recovery. *Now that's star power.*

In the west, they will probably shout and shriek and yell and faint when they see a star. But it ends there. In India they follow, they worship, they all *love* them. But there is a serious threat that this kind of craziness may not be seen in future. See, with coming of these multiplexes, we are whistling less in theaters, we are dancing less in theaters, and thus not getting that feeling of being a part of the movies. Plus, since our economy opened up in 1991, these Americans are entering our country like anything. Spider-man, Bat-man, and that round glassed nerdy looking chap, Harry Potter is winning people over. It's time for our stars to buckle up real quick. After all, these American stars also have a discreet wish to be worshipped.

After the movie when I returned home, Haider was already there. Sober today.

'Not drunk today,' I asked. He had something else in his head.

'Oh my god! You really shaved it off. It was not one of my nightmares.'

'Why, am I not looking good?'

'You are looking good, but it's not about the look. *Why* did you shave it off? Why you had to do such a thing?' Silence in the room for a brief second. 'For that girl, right. Are you a retard or something? What a *fool* you are?' I was shocked and confused to hear that. 'Dude, I am not that religious, in fact I am not into religion at all. I tried quitting alcohol, tried to grow a beard, pray five times a day, keep those fasts. But I was a failure at all that. A complete failure.' He stood up, gnashing his teeth, continued, 'and when you try something and fail at it, either you become jealous and angry at the person who is doing it, or you start respecting him. For you, it was always respect.'

Now this was really making me feel bad. You know, when you try to move on and someone pricks you again, guilt comes back to the fore. Regret takes over. Remorse sets in. It's like somebody is trying to segregate your limbs. It's a pathetic feeling.

'If she really loves you, she would have liked the way you are. As they say, love a person *who loves you,* and not a person *whom you love.* Why you had to shave it off brother? Why did you shave it off Ameen?'

The thing I was scared of, guilt and remorse setting their roots in my heart again, happened. I suddenly started lamenting my decision. I went and again stood in front of the mirror. Touched my cheeks. It's not there. I started running my hands roughly, more roughly. Furiously. Violently. I scratched it again and again. And then tears streamed down my face. And then I ran.

I ran and ran and ran. The rush of my breath could be heard. Not stopping till I reached the mosque again. I went in, and fell down on my knees. I went down on my fours, I remained in a *sajdaa* for the next ten minutes, weeping like a baby. Crying for shaving my beard. For a person whom I had just known for about year and a half, I ditched something which was with me for years. Always with me. I promised I will get it back soon. Very soon.

I had promised that evening that I will see Almighty with that beard on my face. Today is probably the death of my evening. And I am still clean shaved.

"Have no regrets. The elderly usually don't have regrets for what we did, but rather for things we did not do. The only people who fear death are those with regrets."

Most of the great men were of the same opinion. That is, never to regret your decisions and do as you wish and yearn to do. Live your life on your own terms and your will. If that's the case, I never took a wrong decision then.

Bombay is full of liars. You will come across liars everywhere. In your college. At your workplace. In trains and buses. At coffee shops. At gymkhanas. Liars, liars and more liars. Poor liars, rich liars, middle class liars. There are many of them roaming around. But the liars who take the cake are institutes and tuitions who claim that they can teach you English in a span of 30 days. Wow! Now that's what I call a lie. A White lie. A bold lie. Right in your face.

You will see huge hoardings all around you shouting-;
"Is English your problem? Do you get embarrassed when people talk in English with you? Here is the solution. Join our classes. Face the world with a new confidence. Learn English ONLY in 30 days."

Let me tell you, *please don't join them.* They all are a bunch of swindlers. Liars! I learnt it in a decade, and they can teach you in 30 days flat. *Balls!* Nobody's pop can teach you that quick. Not even Charles Dickens. Or Shakespeare.

Though there is one very interesting and a strange fact about these hoardings. Always you will find a green parrot with the reddest possible beak on all these hoardings carrying advertisements of these classes.
As if, the parrot is their brand ambassador. Hell may break lose, but that parrot will always be there, inviting you to master the art of speaking English. Yes, I still consider it to be an art.

Sometime in between Sachin Tendulkar, the same cricketer abba used to praise hell of a lot when I was a kid, scored his 35th international test cricket hundred taking him past Sunil Gavaskar's record and placing him right at the top of the lot. He went on to become the greatest batsmen world ever saw.

Also that year two international cola companies came under the scanner of Centre for Science and Environment, a leading public interest research and advocacy group in India. The study found a cocktail of three to five different pesticides residues in all the samples tested by them - and on an average, the pesticide residues were 24 times higher than those proposed by the Bureau of India Standards, the government body responsible for standardization and quality control. Their study found high levels of: Lindane, Chlorpyrifos, (a neurotoxin) Heptachlor, (which is banned in India completely) and Malathion. All deadly pesticides, powerful enough to kill a man over a hundred times. This was a grave public health scandal. Why do these companies which are globally recognized need to be involved is such horrendous and disgusting practices. Just to make a few quick bucks, they play with the lives of so many people.

Please, officials. Get up and jail these scoundrels. But why will you? Your Swiss account has already been credited. Right!

My bond with Priyanka was getting stronger and stronger with every passing day. Thankfully, terrorists were no more exploding things and neither of her friend's dad was dying. Our basketball cum smoke sessions continued, with movies on the weekends. A few times even without her gang of girls.

But there was another bug which was constantly pinching me. Even if I somehow won Priyanka over, how cheap would it sound when people will talk about a super hot and a super rich girl having an affair with a mere basketball coach. Now I was fine with that cheap tag. But will Priyanka be fine was the question.

And that is when I decided to quit this job and take up something more professional. More respected. You know there is no respect or place for sports like basketball or football in our country. No matter if it's a global sport, or an American sport. We just don't care for any other sport. I had to look for may be something in which I will also be able to go to an office in those trousers and shirts. Some 9 to 5 sort of a job.

Now this was the phase when the whole world was going gaga over India's sudden and gigantic boom in the field of IT and outsourcing. Very rapidly in the early years of the new millennium, many American companies came to our country and opened their offices in cities like Delhi, Bombay. Huge buildings, not made of stones and bricks, but of glasses, came into existence. And things called call centers were born.

When these greedy American companies came over, they needed agents to make calls and take calls. They were hunting desperately for people who can speak English fluently. That was the only criteria to crack their interview. And India is a land full of such jerks, who may not know their national language or any other tongue, but their love for English is unconditional. Though I need to confess, I was also turning into one such jerk. I walked in for a quick round of interview. This time with a proper resume, and cracked it easily. I was a call center *executive* now.

The induction happened and then for the first few months it was all about assorted kinds of trainings. Accent training. Operations training. Process training. Out of all, the accent training was the silliest. In this, they train you how to sound like an American in two weeks' time. How unrealistic and foolish is that. By telling you things like, "Kiss your W's and Bite your V's" they expect that Americans will not come to know that they are speaking to an Indian. Huh! The ultimate goal of all these training session is to teach you "Tricks and Trades of Fooling an American over the Phone."

One of these tricks is not telling them your real name. In a call center you become a John or a Jack or a Don. It's your pseudonym. You are no more a Ram or a Rahim.

Now once your theoretical training and stuff gets over, and you clear a few more very easy rounds of tests, you are all set to hit the floor. Hitting the floor out here means, ready to start business. You start taking-making calls to these Americans. When I went on the floor for the first time, I was left with an open mouth. Gaping.

That place was full of those Tic-Tic machines. You know, computers. There were many of them. Kept on innumerous small terminals attached to one another, one after the other. On every terminal, was a person sitting, with a headset, talking to an American sitting millions of miles away, where the sun must be rising now. It all looked very hotchpotch. Very messy. Like a Persian Bazaar.

The call making procedure was something very different than what I had perceived it to be. We don't make calls manually. It's not done through a telephone set that is at your home or you see hanging in a PCO.

The *computer* makes a call for you. The *computer* disconnects it for you and it is via the *computer* only that you talk across continents. Quite intriguing! My respect for these Tic-Tic machines was constantly growing. I don't know who invented these computers. But whoever it was, 'Dude, your stuff is virtually running the whole world today.'

Call center is a place which works on its own terms. It buzzes with energy at nights, when the whole of Bombay is asleep. But goes lull in the mornings when Bombay is running around. One has to give the credit to call centers for Bombay being called a city which never sleeps.

One needs to be very attentive while on a call. Small things like making sure to empathize with the Americans even when their cat or their dog or their rat or any pet animal dies, had to be kept in head. Most of them would not cry if their wives die, but they will shed tears like anything if their pet animal passes away.

By chance, if you make some ridiculous or silly mistake, or are unable to understand their accent, tell them to kindly repeat their query. It will be your doom. Because the next question he will ask is, "Where are you *located?*" But again we will fool them. We will lie. Instead of telling them that we are sitting in a city called Bombay in a country called India, we will tell them that we are in New York, or California or San Francisco or some place within United States. I repeat, we just don't want them to sniff out that we are *Indians?* That should *just* not happen.

Don't you want to know why we keep fooling them, keep telling a false name and false location. Because if they sniff out that we are Indians, a barrage of abuses and profanity will be hurled at you. The white man will be enraged.

"How the fuck can I, an American, talk to an Indian."

"You bloody Indian, you rascal, you stole my job. My family is dying because your family is eating."

"I am sorry but I would not like to share my information with an Indian. Transfer my call to America."

I fail to understand why they abuse us? If they are so desperate for these jobs, then either create a few jobs in your country, or tell your greedy companies to forget about a few billion dollars they are saving by outsourcing, and take the jobs back to your land.

Or tell your *Mr.* President to put a complete ban on this outsourcing business. Or best, *stop* using credit cards or plastic money. The root cause of these call centers are those plastic cards. Most of the companies out here are debt collection agencies or customer service providers. Stop using them, get rid of us.

But these Americans just can't live without these cards. They live on plastic money. Their white balls will freeze if they step out of their houses without one.

Also, this is where an American and an Indian differs. Suppose a middle class Indian man wants to buy a Bajaj scooter, he will work hard all his life. He will create a small savings account in his bank. Every month he will keep depositing small amounts in that account, specifically created for his scooter. May be in two years or three years' time there will be enough money in the account of his to buy a scooter. He will save all his life to buy what he desires.

Americans don't have that much of patience. If he wants to buy a super-bike, he will straightaway go to the showroom, take out his credit card and will buy a bike then and there itself. And then all his life he will keep paying in small installments. They don't know how to save. They live on credit. They breathe on credit. They pee on credit and they shit on credit.

In one sentence; An Indian *makes small savings* all his life to buy; An American *pays small installments* all his life to buy.

Some of these loafers go fugitive when the time to make the payment arrives. They don't pay their installments, and that is where our role starts. That is, the time when we, Indians put on our headsets and after that long beep, remind the person at the other end, "hey white man, time to pay for the super-bike."

Initially it was difficult. But soon I started liking my job. And surprisingly, Americans too. After all, I was my ammi's son. She always wanted me to go to America. That was not to happen, but at least, I talked to 100 Americans every day. I will tell her soon. There was something similar between both of us. *I and Americans, we both are nasty, spiteful and selfish.* Ha!

I like these Americans for one more reason. They speak English so well. You see, for a man who came from a small town, to speak English was always an art. But for an American, it's not an art, it's *their* language. We Indians may try and learn and master their language, but we will never be able to beat them at it. It's their own stuff. While we have acquired it. Though many of us claim that we speak better English than the Americans. Whenever I hear a person say that, I am forced to say, *"what a fucking joke."*

I also like these Americans because they are good at cooking stories. By that, I don't mean the films and books they have written. But by stories they cook to make sure that they are considered the greatest race on this planet. For example-: when a Newton discovers gravity, he says that the question struck his mind when an apple fell on his head. Wow! And that bozo never noticed that when he was peeing all his life, it was not flying up in the air, but falling on the ground. When he was shitting, sitting on that chair, his crap was falling down, and not forcing its way back into his plump ass.

I think it's all false. Lies. And these Americans are teaching us to lie like them you see. They are scared that the brown man is going to rule the world. They are making us immoral and debauched like them. Why do you think girls in our country are roaming around in mini-mini shorts now. These Americans taught them. Why do you think boys are marrying against their parents' wishes. These Americans taught them. Why do you think boys are marrying boys. I suppose you know who taught them.

At call centers I got to learn a lot of English profanities. After all, although my English was smooth, my accent used to get me in. Every second American used to sniff out that I am a *bloody Indian*. They would abuse. And I would *learn*. I used to behave like a dart board when they used to abuse me. Throw the darts, I will take it all in. After sometime, I consciously used to speak in an Indian accent. I *wanted* them to abuse. Ha!

But the call center can't take all the credit for teaching me English profanities. Half of them, I learnt in one night. In fact, in a gap of two hours. That place was a nightclub. A discotheque. Another great discovery of the mankind I would say. It reveals the true color of these rich men. Let me tell you about that night in detail.

Priyanka and her gang of girls were going to a nightclub in Bandra. Now nightclub is a place where most of the rich-debauched men of this city party. In a nightclub, the system is quite unique. If you go alone, you pay more, if you go as a couple, you pay less. *How stupid?*

Now everyone in her gang had a boyfriend, but Priyanka didn't. She was single. Meant she was not sleeping with anybody, or, what is the difference between a friend and a boyfriend. I was a friend. But I wanted to be a boyfriend. *You getting my hidden intentions.*

So she called me over to visit the nightclub with her. Me and she! *As a couple.* The thought when pondered over, gave me many naughty ideas. I had a pre-conceived notion in my head that a nightclub is a place to booze, score and fuck. I was not interested in the earlier two, but the latter. Time to get lucky with the girl has arrived Ameen. But it all turned out to be a nightmare.

Now that was my first visit to such a place. The first unnerving moment came when I saw Priyanka in her outrageously revealing dress. She looked like those whores I had seen on the Linking road. I lost interest. Next, when I entered, the darkness amazed me. The music playing at an extremely high decibel was ripping apart my ear drums. The strobe lights, extremely flashy lights, going on-off were sending me in a tizzy. Under those psychedelic lights, people all around turn into animated cartoon characters. The smell of alcohol was not making things easy for me. So many girls in so less clothes all around you, jumping, and with them everything on their bodies jumping as well. I started stumbling. I was no more able to stand properly. Sliding, gliding, bumping into people. And then, right then and there, the second half of my coaching for English profanities began.

I took a step forward, bumped into somebody and that somebody yelled, *"Fuck off you jerk."* I took a step back, bumped into someone else, that someone else barked, *"dumbfuck."* I went right, *"pervert."* Back, *"Asshole, Dickhead, You fuck in the head."*

So I can assure you, if you want to learn English profanities, join a call center and speak in an Indian accent. Or visit a nightclub and bump into people. You will master the art of abusing people in English. Make sure you bump into a nightclub, because if you bump somewhere else, that mother-fucker will turn into a *madar-chod.* See, though we Indians know this American language, it has somewhat turned into a showoff kind of a stuff. So in a nightclub, nobody will abuse in Hindi, but in English. Nightclub is a place to show off.

Let me tell you one more thing. Because I am experienced and have learnt these English abuses from two schools, from Indians and from Americans, the profanities these Indians taught me were 'oh so yesterday.' So old. Even a few rickshaw drivers may know them. The abuses hurled at me from Americans were really nice. They sounded like profanities. And that is where my belief gets stronger that we Indians can never speak English as well as them. Remember, it's not art for them. It's their language.

With suddenly more money and more English profanities in my kitty, and a new look on my face, I was more confident than ever before. There was no need to look at the ground while walking or while eating at the canteen, or while sitting in lectures. I was almost at par with the shaved rascals. All I didn't have was a girlfriend. Didn't I just now tell you the difference between a friend and a girlfriend. The reason for my agony was, Priyanka was still a friend.

Now it all happened in a very quick succession. The beard going off, vanishing of pleated trousers, carrying a much fatter wallet, and Priyanka becoming a close friend. It all obviously had some adverse effect. Effect on the people around me. The shaved rascals were jealous. Like those kids in my school got jealous the day they found out that I come to school in a car, likewise.

Now one day, they tried to play with me. A group of rascals sitting around me were in a mood for some fun that day. But I was no more scared of them. Or conscious of myself. I stayed on.

'Man, have you done anything with Priyanka?' One of them said, displaying all his teeth and banging the desk with his steel watch.

'What are you doing with Priyanka then man? Introduce me to her. I will teach you what one needs to do with a girl?' I tried to recall best of profanities I had learnt.

'Or man are you a homosexual. Your pee-pee goes out for men.' I looked at him, placed my hand over his, not letting him bang the desk with his steel watch anymore.

'You really feel I am a homosexual. Send over your mother for one night to my place, and you will come to know after nine months if I am a homosexual. And do let me know if you have a kid brother, or a kid sister. Ready to cut a deal dear. So tonight, I and your mother will do some...' I moved my waist back and forth.

The whole gang got up, ready to tear me into pieces. Luckily, the professor arrived and they had to sit back. I knew I can't afford to sit till the lecture gets over, for they will then

Love, Lust & Lies

pounce on me like hungry cannibals. I gave professor an excuse and left midway. I walked till the door and turned around. Rascal and his friends were still staring me, I moved my waist again, smiled and walked off.

I don't know how much these rascals like the word "man." They use it as a suffix in every sentence. Some rough examples:

'Was sup *man!*'

'That's awesome *man.*'

'Yeah *man!*'

'Shit *man!*'

'Cool *man!*'

'What the *fuck* is this man, *man?*'

Honestly, I feel the use of this slang is so yesterday. Those niggers or mostly rap artists in the west use that quite often. We simply "cut-copy-paste" whatever they do. May it be movies, or may it be language, may it be the American lifestyle, we are copying it all. When looked deeply, somewhere, it's a threat. A threat which can make us slaves again.

Do you remember the Gurkha guard at Priyanka's house. It was time for him to salute me from now on. I had jumped one more caste in the hierarchy. I was now a guest, not a coach. I was now a friend and no more some mere employee. In jeans and T-shirts I was also looking like one of her rich friends. I was working in nights and sleeping in days now. Thus, my college was more or less not witnessing my sexy face. Priyanka called in one day, enquiring about my job.

She said she was no more playing basketball. No partner you see. Actually she was missing me. That is what my corrupted mind told me. One day she asked me to come to her place at eight at night as my shift started at eleven. I thought for a second and agreed.

Love, Lust & Lies

You noticed that one second my mind wasted after she invited me to her place. You know what was I thinking in that one second. Something really wicked and mischievous. "Why is she calling me over to her place at night. Has the time to become her boyfriend arrived."

If I survive today, and somehow somebody saves my life, I promise I will write a whole book on this alone. *"From friend to boyfriend."* *Uff!* It takes hell lot of a time and money.

Anyways, I reached her building sharp at eight. I also got a pack of sweets wrapped up for her mother. Actually I was a bit dicey of that lady. Mrs. Khanna. How will she react to see a basketball coach coming to meet her daughter. Though I was a call center *executive* now. But the coach tag, servant tag, coolie tag is not that easy to shed. Even if Rajnikanth is a huge star now, people do say that he was just a bus conductor once, you see.

Her apartment was on the 21st floor. I took the lift, it closed with a *ting,* and then it opened with a *ting.* Another great discovery by mankind. I walked out, took a deep breath and then rang the bell. A cuckoo started singing. Kooouuuh, Kooouuuh! Kooouuuh! In my town a bell *rings,* here it *sings.* Wow! Big people. Big city.

Mrs. Khanna opened the door and welcomed me in. I handed over the wrapped gift I had bought with so much *love* and *affection.*
That was a joke. The love and affection part. Ha!
She took it with a huge smile and called out Priyanka. As usual, she came and hugged me straight. I was quite used to it now, the ways and laws of Bombay. Mrs. Khanna was setting up the table. She asked me if I would like to eat something. Though I wanted to, I lost all interest when I saw the table and the cutlery

on it. The rich sit on the table to have dinner, but seems like they are all set for a war.

Big spoons, small spoons, knives, forks, chopsticks, toothpicks. Phew! And then what do they do? They eat just a wee bit. Pineapples, salad and juice. Can you believe that? Sometimes I used to wonder, they are stinking rich, but do they just eat pineapples and salad?

Then the case is no different in the mornings. They take newspapers, magazines, journals and god knows what all, and end up shitting just a wee bit. Now don't question me how do I know that they shit just a wee bit. Obviously, when a man would *eat* a wee bit, he would *shit* only a wee bit.

Once I turned down Mrs. Khanna's offer, Priyanka said, 'come, we will go and sit in the balcony of my room.' Ameen, you were right, it's time to be her boyfriend now. Just to make sure that we will be alone, I asked, 'Is aunty not going to sit and chat with us?'

'Why will aunty sit with us? What has she got to do?' *Right, what has she got to do.* 'Anyways, she goes for a walk early in the mornings, It's time for her to go to bed now.'

Now that relieved me. She goes for a morning walk. Means, she is also debauched. All rich & debauched go for a walk. Mrs. Khanna herself must be sleeping around with her gym trainer or someone of that sort, why will she care if her daughter sleeps with a basketball coach. And a basketball coach is any day better than a gym trainer. Huh!

We crossed her room and went out in the balcony. And then I saw one of the most amazing views of my life. Better than those white peaks in Nainital. My God. *No, Priyanka didn't get naked you scoundrel. I know what you are thinking. You must be a rich man's son. Debauched!*

The aerial view of the city blew me over. It was an eye candy. To stand there and watch the city from there. The whole Bombay, lying there, right in front of you. The view was spellbinding, marvelous.

There are so many lights in Bombay. It gives you an adrenaline. Light have always done that to me. It all looks like gold. Glittering gold. Shining gold.

That is the place where you can actually know what defines Bombay's energy. Even on the 21st floor, there is a constant distant ZZZZ sound, sound of a car honking, or some sound in the background. That constant ZZZZ. Somewhere far, somewhere there.

And beyond that, where these lights end, and where it looks like the sky and those lights and buildings kiss each other, my town is somewhere there. I was to go back to my town in a few days' time. On a small vacation. Almost after three years, I was going back for the first time. This thought somewhat unnerved me. I forgot that I was here to become her boyfriend.

'I am going back home in a few days' time Priyanka, but I am a little worried. How would abba react to find that I shaved. I don't know how will I face him?'

'Do you regret that you shaved it off?' I didn't know the honest answer to this. But still, considering the situation, knew the correct one.

'No. I don't.'

'Then it ends here. You don't need to be worried. Don't regret. I wouldn't have lived my life the way I did if I was going to worry about what people were going to say.' She placed her palm on mine. 'Your abba will understand.'

How easily she said that, "*your abba will understand*." There is a lot of difference between an *abba* and a *daddy* Priyanka. You only know the daddy part. Abba part is much more difficult to handle. I looked back at this magnum opus city, to forget abba and my town. I looked at those cars. I looked at those buildings, slums, malls, a passing train somewhere far, a passing aero-plane in the sky. I looked at the whole of Bombay, then again to the point where the buildings were kissing the skies. I instantly raised my hands up in the air, above my head and showed my middle fingers. Both of them. I yelled.... 'This is for my town. Fuck you. Small people. Small town. Small thinking. Fuck you all. Ameen Jalal is a city dweller now. A citified and a dignified man. A gentleman.'

I showed my middle finger and cursed my town till I was convinced that I have cursed it enough. When I stopped and turned to face Priyanka. She was smiling. I tell you, all rich people are debauched. They all love profanity.

"False words are not only evil in themselves, but they infect the soul with evil."

SOCRATES

This is the only quotation in this book I don't agree with. Or rather I don't want to agree with. Profanity, or false words, as Socrates puts it in, is also like a cigarette. It calms you down.

Soon I was on a train. Going back to my town. A tad nervous, a tad excited. Nervous, I told you why. Excited, going back *home* after long will do that to anybody. Because I was a call center executive now, I would have not done justice to my status if I had traveled back in a second class general coach. I got my reservation done in a first class compartment. AC.

I wanted to check what it is like to travel behind those tinted glasses. To be honest. *It's no fun.* Similarly like watching a movie in a multiplex, it's such a bore to travel in an AC compartment. They provide you blankets, they provide you mattresses, pillows, keep asking you if you want something to eat. Pamper you big time. After all, you pay some 1500 bucks. But it's nothing like traveling in a second class general compartment.

See, first thing is that people in there are neither rich, nor poor. They belong to the most interesting class, the middle class. Now these people neither smell of sweat, nor do they use a fragrance of a famous brand. It's difficult to smell them out. And if I can't smell people, then it really disturbs me. I don't know what to make out of them.

Second, unlike a general bogie, people don't keep on getting down at every station to buy snacks or fill their bottles with tap water. They drink mineral water. Now that's really stupid. They don't know that those bottles also contain the same tap water. The urchins are very smart. They collect the used bottles, fill them up with the tap water and sell them back. I am not stupid. I still got down at every station and kept on filling and refilling my bottle. Please note the way I am speaking now, *"I am not stupid."* This is a new arrogance I have developed. Last time it was not there. Money does that to everybody. I was much robust, behaving like an effendi, full of inane attitude.

Third, the people out here are a lot more educated than me. They talk about politics, religion, and every other stuff I don't know a fuck about. They carry thick books and thick glasses with them. Like this old uncle sitting in front of me. Though, there will always be nice girls around to watch. The beauty of the girl will always be directly proportional to the age of her old man. The older the father, the hotter the girl. All are intellectuals in there, and I don't like intellects. I like geniuses. These morons are book smart, I like street smarts.

But the fourth point really takes the cake. See, may it be a rich man, a poor man, or a middle class man. An intellectual, a foolish or a genius, everybody's digestive system functions the same way. And they all fart. But when a man farts in a general class, the effect fades out soon. Trust me, it doesn't in an AC compartment. It holds on. It takes you by your neck. The whole section of the bogie which has come under the radar of the smell goes silent for those horrendous 5-10 minutes. All eyes look at you, and you look back at all those eyes. Suspicious eyes. "Is he the one." "Or is that bastard the one." A general class is much better. I will return in the general class. This AC is no good for me. Fuck the call center executive tag.

But one thing is common between the two classes. The ticket-checker over here as well goes around with his head stamped: "For-Sale."

So after experiencing the AC stuff, it was time to meet my old friend. My town. The train tiptoed inside the one platform station. I picked up my luggage. The same uncle, the thick glass one, cried, 'you live *here*. You are getting down *here*.' Now that stress on *here*, miffed me. I wanted to say, "Yes you intellectual bastard, half of your country men live *here* and at other such places. You foolish nerd, you read so many books and you don't know this." Obviously I didn't say that, but I wanted to hit back. I did something else. I gave his hot daughter a lewd smile, and just before moving out, bit my lower lips with my upper set of teeth. I raped her with my eyes. Exactly like Haider did with those whores.

The train came to a halt and I jumped out. I was back in my town. I reframed it, I was back in my *abba's* town. I belong to Bombay now. I am a citified, dignified gentleman now. Ha!

I looked around. Everything around looked so slow. So dull. Dying things. I felt so sorry, so bad for the people of my town. They don't know what is life. What it is to live on the 21st floor of a building. Or to drink and dance in a nightclub. Or how sensational is a feeling to have so many sexy girls in short dresses around you. They absolutely lead an unenlightened life.

It felt like I was no more in the same country. By no means or measures one can say that Bombay and my town falls in the same country. In fact, even in the same continent perhaps. These two places are as different as chalk and cheese. These are actually two different worlds. One running around like a whore looking for business. The other one always lying around like a whore who have just been humped. So many years have passed by, but the weather, the atmosphere, the smell, the platform, even the vendor selling tea and coconut biscuits, all were the same. Nothing changes in a town. These people hate changes. They just let everything be.

I moved my eyeballs looking around for abba. And there he was. Also the same. Exactly like I saw him the last time at the same platform. In a *kurta-pajama*, above his ankles and that skull cap intact on his head. Chewing tobacco. He had a larger belly and was moving much slower now though. He had become more lethargic now I suppose. Along with him, was my ammi. In that black veil. The same veil which makes her look like a black haunted figure.

I greeted both of them, hugged them. Ammi moved her hands on my cheeks, again and again. Noticing that something was missing. They were smoother and slicker than before. 'You shaved.' She murmured. I didn't utter a word. She then casually looked at abba. Abba didn't utter a word. I picked up my bag and we walked out of the platform. Till date, I don't know how abba felt when he noticed my shaved beard. He never mentioned anything, and I never gave him an opportunity either. I was kind of happy that he never asked. But at times curiosity used to take over and I used to ponder over the question-: why didn't abba ever ask me the reason for shaving off the beard? I don't know.

The same old red Maruti 800 was waiting for me. Maruti also had aged a bit. The ride was no more smooth as before. Upholstery on the seats also torn at several places. Abba opened the locks and the car swallowed us all in. Ammi then removed her veil and looked at me again. Slipped her fingers across my cheeks again. Then noticed my new attire.

'Jeans and shirt.' Scanned me for a second more, then quipped again, 'look at you, you are looking *exactly* like an American now.' I smiled. Had to happen. Talking with 100 Americans every day. Had to happen.

Our car zipped across the market, my madrasa, my school, the old theater. It was all the same. Took a turn and entered the lane in which my house was waiting for me.

Finally, in the true sense of the word, I was back home. No matter how much you hate the town, the dying things around, the slothful people around, one will never have any complaints from his own house. The feeling is extremely joyful. Peaceful. Or else, why do the birds return to their own trees and own nests every evening. Nature also knows the importance of a home. Returning home gives you that extra piece of mind.

Ammi had cooked *haleem* that day. For the third time in her life. *I hope you remember the first two times. I don't have enough time in my hands to repeat that. The blood is dripping down real quick from my neck now. I can be dead anytime.*

Ammi sat next to me, filling my plate persistently. While abba sat on that famous rickety armchair of his, with the beads. Eyes on that neem tree. Now when will that neem tree fall. My god. It's really difficult to even imagine what my abba tries to find in that stupid tree. Some great-great-great grandfather of mine planted that. If I would have been alive then, knowing that this tree will make my abba a sloth, I would have chopped that great-great-great grandfather's hand, so that this tree could never have been planted. What a waste of time. Huh!

'You know, there is someone who has been enquiring about your return incessantly. Literally pestered me.' I didn't have any idea whom she was talking about. The aroma and flavor of haleem in my nose and on my tongue was too consuming. I kept on eating.

'Go and meet her in the evening. Zareen will be so glad to see you.' I instantly came to a standstill.

Zareen! She was talking about Zareen and I didn't notice. *The haleem must have been really nice.* But when she finally did mention her name, the aroma from my nose and the flavor from my tongue, all went away. How the fuck could I forget her. My oldest, closest friend was waiting for me.

After the lunch I switched on the Television. They were talking about yet another terrorist attack in Varanasi in which at least 15 people died and more than 50 were injured. Also about the medical doctors who started strike against central government decision on reservation for OBC (other backward classes) in medical institution.

Naushad, the genius music composer died that year. Carter road in Bombay was renamed as "Sangeet Samrat Naushad Ali road."

It was quite displeasing to know about such terrorist attacks every other day. News channels are one such displeasing place. Nothing pleasant up there. I switched it off. Glad that I was not in Bombay giving Priyanka a chance to abuse me. My gaze fell at the verandah outside, and memories rushed in. I and Zareen used to play day in and day out in that verandah. Sometimes with the goats and sometimes only two of us. Sometimes with the old truck tyre, sometimes collecting the berries. I was about to get up and leave to meet her when abba enquired about his dearest possession he had given me to take care of.

'Ameen, have you kept my golden diary safe and sound?'

'Yes! It's absolutely fine.'

'Can you please get that. I want to see it.' I went in my room, and came back with it. Abba's face gleamed up, the shimmering cover doing its trick. I was glad that at least he was not watching that silly tree.

'How did you find the quotes inside?' And then answered himself. 'I know they are great. All my childhood.......' *You know that, don't you.* He repeats the same things over and over again. Watches the same tree over and over again. At times abba is unbearable.

'But tell me, which one is your favorite. The best according to you.' I knew my answer straightaway. Still acted, squinted my eyes, and then said, 'False words are not only evil in themselves, but they infect the soul with evil. By Socrates.'

Abba smiled at me. I smiled back.

False words. Ha!

What abba didn't notice behind that sly smile of mine was the fact that I know so many of these false words that I can make a thicker diary of them than this golden diary of his. I would name it, "The Asshole Diary" with Hitler's or Stalin's picture on the cover. I moved out of the house, ready to meet Zareen.

I crossed the fence exactly in the same fashion I used to do as a child. It all looked like life had come a full circle for me. I was now in Zareen's compound. I entered her house. There was nobody around. A steel glass fell making a shrill noise, breaking the monotony. A black cat rushed passed. Quite spooky. Zareen has moved on, from goats to cats, I thought.

I clicked my fingers and clucked my tongue, trying to catch the attention of what looked like only living thing in that house. Instead of running in my arms, the cat ran in the opposite direction. A door was left ajar, she sneaked in. I ran behind her. Thumped open the door and saw the cat sitting pretty in somebody's lap now. That somebody was Zareen. She turned almost in a reflex, calling out, 'Who is it?' A long silence after that. She looked at me, I looked at her.

'It's me, Ameen.' Wearing a white cotton salwar-kameez sans the dupatta, her cleavage showing clearly. She sat there like that, mute, watching me transfixed. I stood there mute, watching her. Probably the cat meowed breaking the monotony once again.

The purr of the cat getting her back, she quickly picked up her dupatta and draped it around her neck.

'You are back.' She stood up. Came forward and gave me a closer look. 'Jeans and T-shirt. You are looking like those filmy heroes. You are looking so different.'

'So are you.' I could not take my eyes off her. She had turned out into one beautiful girl. Or maybe my way of noticing girls had changed. She was fuller, mature with a lissome figure and many times beautiful than when we last met. I noticed she was wearing a bra under her salwar as well. I was not sure if she used to wear one before. I was glad something has changed in my town. And that too changed positively.

'Ammi and abba are not here. They are out of town for some cousin's wedding. They would have been so happy to see you.' We went out in the living room.

'Are you not happy to see me?' I asked her. A discreet smile graced her face. I was good at noticing these things now. Bombay taught me quite well.

'Of course I am.' She started preparing tea for us. And then served it with some jaggery.

'So, how is Bombay. How is your college?'

'Bombay is fast, always running, college is fun, full of girls....and boys of course.' She bit into her jaggery.

'Lots of girls are there.' Her face expressionless.

'Lots of.'

'Do they all dress like as they show in films.'

'Yeah! Pretty much. Most of them wear jeans and shirts and skirts. Mini shorts as well.'

'How do they look?'

'You want an honest answer. They are not my type.' The discreet smile back on her face. That was actually a lie. I am too good at lying you see. But that lie made her feel good. And that made me feel good.

'What all has Bombay taught you?'

'That rains and girls of Bombay are unpredictable.' Her smile much clearer now. But her urge to know more about the girls hadn't died yet.

'None of the girls wear salwar-kameez in your college?'

'They are not beautiful enough to look good in a salwar-kameez. After all everybody can't be as beautiful as you, right.'

And she blushed. And then hesitatingly asked, 'and did you fall in love with somebody?'

'How can I fall in love with somebody when I am already in love with somebody.'

With that her cheeks turned red as an apple. Shy, she excused herself to get some more jaggery. Opened the flask and while her hands did the needful, her mouth kept on asking questions.

'Ameen, I was thinking if we can go for a movie once again. Together. I mean, ammi-abba are also not here, so why not ...' I was not in a mood to catch a movie again in that gory theater. Multiplexes do have their own charms you see.

'Unh, Zareen, I have some urgent work today. Not possible.' Her face turned grim once again, hands no more searching for jaggery.

'I haven't been to that theater since *that* day. I thought maybe when you will return I will go once again.' I didn't want to disappoint her.

'I said not possible *today*. How about tomorrow? Afternoon show?'

'Yeah sure. I am fine with any show.' Brought the jaggery and sat on her seat once again.

I then took out a small packet out from my pocket.

'Here, this is for you.' That was a bracelet. Every day I used to see dozens of girls buying that stuff on hill road. I bought one for her just before leaving, at the eleventh hour.

'Is this for me?' Her eyes glittering with delight. Agape. She wore it around her slender arms. Then kept praising it for hours.

'You did think of me sometimes. Didn't you.'

'How many times did you think of me?' I bounced the question back.

'Go count the stars.'

'I can't.'

'I can't either.'

Next day right after lunch I went back to Zareen's house. It was one of those rare incidences where I had taken enough care to keep my promise. Actually I didn't want to lose this opportunity of spending some more time with Zareen. She was already sitting in her veil, ready to leave.

'Oh, there you are. You will go in this *veil*.'

'Obviously, if someone catches me with you, I will be crucified. You forgot what happened last time.' We started walking for the theater. Me, in jeans and shirt with a burqa clad girl. The pair didn't quite look right to me.

'Do you always come out of your house under this black cover.'

'Yup! Ammi-abba will not approve of me loitering around without this.' I nodded.

'You know, I am wearing a new dress today. And have also styled my eyes with kohl.' She was very chirpy that afternoon.

'I can't see it. Where is it?'

'Stupid. It's inside this veil *na*. I will show you in the theater.'

'How inane is that. One can't look at his own nails in a theater. It's so dark out there. You forgot or what. Show it to me *now*.'

'Don't talk like a child. I can't remove it here.'

'Then I am not taking a step further. I will not move till you take that thing off.'

'Ameen, try to understand.'

'Do you care more about this silly world, or do you care more about me. If you care for me, then you will remove it right away, or else. I am not going.' I turned my back on her. And when I turned to face her again, she had already taken it off.

'Don't question me if I care for you or not ever again.'

That was the thing with Zareen. She would cover any lengths and breadths for me. She was wearing a *churidar* salwar-kameez. A kind of a body fit dress. Looking stunning and more. The kohl in her eyes, hair tied cleanly. Her white cheeks again turned red. That is the difference between a hot siren babe of my college and this beautiful damsel of my town. One leaves you with lust, while the other one just leaves you with a desire to look more and more.

'Now can we quickly go please. You are going to get me killed one day.'

We started moving again. I could feel that she was extremely nervous. Her heart beats thumping, arms trembling, eyeballs looking everywhere, lips moving silently. I drifted closer to her and held her hands. She looked at me and strapped her fingers tight. We walked till the theater, in absolute silence.

When we reached the cinema hall, we were unpleasantly surprised. That old theater no more used to play decent movies. It had turned into a den. A den where soft porn movies, B grade movies, which are full of sex and murders were played. The poster said; "*Pyaasi Padosan* - Thirsty Neighbor." Now, going to watch such stuff with Zareen could have caused much embarrassment.

'Do they play nice movies anywhere in this town. Decent movies, family movies, Shah Rukh Khan movies.' I asked a passerby.

'For that you will have to go to the other theater. Take a right from that lane. There they play decent movies.' His eyes were all the time on Zareen and hands on his groin. He came closer to me, whispered in my ears, 'who goes to watch a decent film with a beautiful girl like that. Go, watch this one, if you want I can give you the tickets half the rate.'

'No, I am fine. I will go watch that decent one.'

'Are you sure?' I nodded, he patted my back, showing me his tobacco stained teeth. We walked away. He shouted, 'if your mood swings in Pyaasi Padosan's favor, I am here. Buy tickets from me. Okay!'

'Okay!' I shouted back. I and Zareen broke into a discreet guffaw.

We took the turn as instructed and reached another theater. A new one. "Regal Talkies" written on the face of the building. Now this was not a multiplex, but a new stand alone hall. The movie we went for starred superstar Hrithik Roshan. The name was *Krishh*.

It was good to watch a movie with people whistling all around you, dancing to the tunes and gaping in amazement when the protagonist kicked the antagonist by leaping and jumping from buildings in an impossible fashion. So much of entertainment just for a mere sum of 50 rupees. Kind of entertainment no multiplex can provide you.

But some real drama was waiting to unfold after the movie. We were walking back, she still not wearing her veil, hands in my hands.

'You know what Zareen. There was a girl in the hall, who looked exactly like a girl who was there in my madrasa. Look how time flies by. There we were small kids of....' Zareen let her hands fall free of my hold. Stood firm in her place. I turned around.

'What happened?'

'I thought there were no girls in your madrasa.'

It took some time to realize what she meant by that statement. An old lie, a very old lie of mine had just returned to haunt me. I was left speechless, ashamed suddenly.

'Why you had to lie then Ameen?'

'I was just a kid then Zareen.'

'A kid. But mature enough to understand such things.' She pointed her index finger, 'you are equally responsible of robbing me of my education. You are equally responsible for my illiteracy. You never wanted me to be at par with you. Isn't it?' She was absolutely right. As a kid I had been very hostile and rude with this girl. Though she always had been sweeter than sugar and probably loved me since then.

I stood there like a drone. Like a thief who has just been caught red hand. She wore her veil. Went past me. The kohl now acting as a pollutant, turned the tears rolling down her cheeks black.

'You know that I have always liked you. Don't you.' I yelled with a husk in my voice. She turned back. Looked at me for one last time before flipping the cloth covering her face.

'I have always loved you.' She didn't pay any heed, left me there, deserted.

And then probably for the first time in my life, tears rolled down my cheeks as well. I had done that to her so many times, today she returned the favor. I felt aghast, broken and extremely angry at myself. I took out a pen from my pocket, placed it between my index and middle fingers, and pressed it hard. As the mullahs used to punish in my madrasa. Punishing you for committing some err. I used to be pained then. But today I didn't feel any pain. The pain of watching Zareen go like that was much bigger to sustain.

Not understanding what to do, I turned away and walked wherever my legs carried me to. I wandered around. I went to the market. Watched women buying groceries. Kids running around. A constable picked up a pack of cigarette from a shop without caring to pay in return. A crippled beggar begging around. I crossed the market soon and was now again standing in front of the old theater. Outside that tacky, non air conditioned, single screen cinema hall, or as they are called, talkies. I was observing the poster of the movie running inside. A dusky woman, with a golden wig, giving an illusion of a blonde, in a two-piece black outfit. Big tits begging to pop out. A man, bare-chested, lusting for her. The font bold and loud, announcing the arrival of *'Pyaasi Padosan'*

Next, I observed the crowd. This crowd, which forms the giant mass of our population. This crowd, which forms the major junk of our population. The *'chawanni class'* audience, as Haider used to call them. All smelly, looking as if haven't shaved for months. Eyes red and tired. Rugged clothes, some only in vests. Silver chain lockets around their necks, every now and then adjusting their under garments. Waiting for the shutter to open, so that their date in the dark, with the *Pyaasi Padosan* can begin.

'You are back. The charm of Pyaasi Padosan is not easy to evade. Do you want a ticket. Fifteen rupees,' he said, showing his stained teeth, 'lots of fun,' he added. He was the same man. I asked for one ticket.

'You alone. Where is the item you were with.' He gave a half smile. 'Without her the fun will be reduced to half.' I gave him an intent look, snatched the ticket and went in.

The condition of the hall was horrible. It looked like there had been no fresh air in that place for the last 25 years. The smell was so foul, probably there were a dozen mice lying dead. The walls which were once white, were now red. Courtesy, the great *paan* lovers. The toilets hadn't been cleaned since India got independent. The screen torn in four places. I sat surrounded by coolies, prostitutes, rickshaw drivers, waiters who serve in small *udipi* restaurants, etc. *Desi* Romeos kissing their *desi* Juliets. Educated, honest, respectable people are nowhere to be seen in these places. They cannot go in. The seats are torn. The AC is not there. The person in the next seat will try to pore them in.

But I didn't care. I am no less than these shoddy and dodgy characters. I am worse. I am one of them. The protagonist of that soft porn film was screwing two ladies at the same time. His own wife in the mornings and his "thirsty neighbor" in the evenings. In the climax, his wife kills him for his infidelity. In these movies the law of the jungle is followed. Like they do in those gulf countries. A hand for a hand and an eye for an eye.

This is what happens with liars. They are punished brutally. Zareen did no wrong. She holds all the rights to love me or leave me. I was rightly responsible for her illiteracy.

It was my last day in town. I was all set to leave for Bombay the coming day. I was glad. Nothing exciting was left for me out here. My own house was looking like an ominous figure, as if coming to eat me. I tried to meet Zareen a few times, but she didn't open the door of her room. I gave up. I was pretty sure that I won't be able to see her probably ever again, till ammi gave me some heartening news.

'I haven't prepared lunch for you today,' Ammi said. I gave her a perplexed look.

'Zareen called up. She has invited you over lunch. She has cooked *yakhni pulao* for you. Go and meet her. She must be waiting.'

Now if girls of Bombay are unpredictable, girls of town are no less. Erratic, fickle, impulsive, volatile. I don't know what.

Actually it's not about a city or a town. This caste, female caste, is in itself impossible to understand. Till now she was not willing to talk to me. And now suddenly, she calls me over for lunch.

I went over. She was setting up the table. Placing the dishes, plates and glasses.

'Hi!' She turned to me. Looking stressed.

'Hi. How are you?' She asked in a meek voice.

'Bad. Very bad.' I noticed she didn't cover her cleavage today. Her *dupatta* still lying on the sofa near the table. I noticed her beautiful feet, walking around without any slippers or stuff.

'Are you angry?' I asked.

'I was. But can I be angry with you for long.' That was relieving. I sat down. She picked up the porcelain dish and stood above my right shoulder to serve me some. Her breasts almost in my face. A very difficult position to sit in.

She then said, 'I will just go and take a quick shower. You enjoy your meal.'

Is she trying to seduce me. What is she up to? I sat there with various such questions bouncing in my head, feeding myself.

The bathroom was in a corner in the same hall. I could hear ruffling sounds of her clothes being taken off. Now goes the top. Now the salwar. Now the undergarments. Is she naked inside. Is she....

I noticed a keyhole. The very next moment my right eye was closed and left eye was inside the keyhole.

Yes. She had completely stripped. I saw her curves, her hips, her legs. Drops rolling down smoothly. Making different paintings using her body as a canvas. Suddenly the shower stopped. I rushed back and sat still. Minutes later she emerged dressed. Hair wet, face clean. Looked at me. Poker faced, yet a trace of a thin smile could be easily figured out. Opened her palm, and placed the key intact in the keyhole. Did she know? Did she do this purposely?

Breaking the silence which was kind of gagging us, I asked, 'can I get some water?' She walked up with the jug, breasts again in my face. Her wet tresses left her upper arm and neck soaked. Pouring the water into the glass she asked, 'Were you lying when you said that?'

'What did I say?' She didn't change her position. Knew it's effective.

'That you love me.' I stopped feeding myself. Looked at her.

'Do *you* think I was lying?' She looked in my eyes deeply. For full one minute. Placed the jug back on the table. Moved forward.

And then she held my face. And then she kissed me. I kissed her back and we both kissed each other back. Fresh tears emerged in her eyes, but we kept kissing. She was almost crying and kissing at the same time. My hands moved below her salwar, dug in her butt. She moved away. I pulled her closer. My chest rubbing against hers. She moved her face away. Our bodies still joint in the middle though.

'You were always with me, in my heart. Even when you were miles away from here. I always missed you.' She cried some more.

'The mirror on the wall reflected your face, not mine. Every night just before I would fall asleep, my flicking eyes searched for you.' She cried some more.

'These lips of mine never failed to mention your name once.' Cried some more.

God! She had practiced. She had rehearsed.

Love, Lust & Lies

'Will you marry me?' I was not interested in any of her poetic lines. Panting now, I tried biting her lips once again. She offered her neck.

'No! Will you marry me?' By now, my want had turned into a need.

'Of course I will. I have loved you.' A few more fresh tears emerged and she kissed me again. Deeply. Our throats dry now. I decided to take the next step. I tried removing her top. She held my hand.

'We must get married first. Come, we will get married right away. I know a *Qazi*.'

Now this shook me a little. But still not good enough to get me out of her domination.

'We will, for sure. But later.' She drifted away from me. The void space between us invoking me to go for her once again.

'I don't have time Ameen. I haven't told you something.'

I filled the space once again. I licked her neck, tried going deep under, she didn't allow.

'I am engaged. I will be married soon.' This time I moved away. 'By the time you come back, I will be gone. We need to marry right away.' She kept touching my face at regular intervals, making sure that her effect doesn't die out. She gripped my face in her palms, and gazed in my eyes.

'Let's go for the *nikaah*. Now! I was always yours. I can't live without you.' I stayed shut. She tapped her forehead against mine. Held me, hugged me tight, choked and kept on begging me to marry her. She then held my hand and placed it on her breasts. I slipped. That was what you say is a master-move.

'Let's go,' I said. And then she giggled, cried, kissed, all at the same time. I was kind of hypnotized.

When evening fell, we left for the Qazi's house. She had definitely prepared it all. The Qazi made us sit on a mat on the ground and then started carrying out the formalities. She covered her head with the dupatta. It was then when I realized that I have actually said yes to marry her. Nervousness gripped me. She noticed that, placed her palm on my palm.

'Do you, Ameen Jalal, son of Muqarram Jalal accept Zareen Rehman as your wife.' I didn't answer. The Qazi repeated. Zareen looked at me, hissed, 'I swear I won't be able to live without you.' Her face still grim and sad, an expression I have always hated to see on that face. I threw caution to the winds and dared to say it. 'I do.'

"A woman wears her tears like jewelry," Abba probably wrote these lines keeping ammi in mind, I hold this for Zareen.

Love, Lust & Lies

16th

A married Ameen returned to Bombay. Though my marriage was still a hush-hush thing, only in the eyes of God, and not on paper or in the eyes of the law. I was glad it was under wraps. But the scary part was that for town people marriage matters only in the eyes of the god. Law... well who cares for.

A marriage can be discarded, a bride can be send back by her in-laws or burnt alive, if it's just on paper. But will be undeniable if in front of a Qazi or a Pandit.

I met Zareen just before sitting in my Maruti, promised to return after my graduation and ask for her hand from her parents. She had given an extremely pleasant and a relieved smile. Her face as fresh as a spring morning.

Back in Bombay, life was running as usual. Time never stops here. You get married, you rape, you die, you kill, do whatever fuck you want to, but nobody will care a fuck for you. They are not bothered about anybody else's business, but theirs. And why should be they? It's good in a way. Which is not the case with my town. Towns are full of intruders. You rape, the whole town will gather to rape you back. You marry, the whole town will be there to eat. You gossip, the whole town will be there to gossip with you.

I came back to my room, unpacked my stuff and picked up my cell phone. Switched it on and it went mad. Messages kept pouring in. One after the other. Half of them were from these mobile networks. Assorted services, tariff plans, silly caller tunes, etc. Other half were from the hot babe. I tell you, her messages were sillier than those tariff plans and caller tunes. First one, she was enquiring about my return, then asking to get something for her, then giving me lots of love, hugs and kisses, missing me loads.

Then calling me her cootchie coo, her sweety pie, her knight in shining armor and god knows what all. *Girls can honestly be stupid, silly and excruciating at times.*

While replying to her messages, I suddenly got trapped in the chains of my conscience. I got a bit scared. A bit mystified. *I am a married man now. How the hell can I be friends with some other girl. I can't do this.*

Sure when I was leaving I was quite attracted to her. May be it was love. Or maybe it was infatuation. Or maybe something else. But now I must end it here. "It ends here Ameen. You will no more see Priyanka. Is that clear." "Yes sir! That's clear." I told myself. I sighed and cleared the message. I kept the phone on my lap, closed my eyes, tired. The phone suddenly started singing at length. Giving me a mild jolt and disturbing my short nap. I grabbed the phone. It read: "Priyanka Calling."

I didn't pick it up. It sang again. I didn't pick it up. This continued for a while. The room was dark and quiet. The only thing making noise was my singing cell phone. A few very tiny insects moved towards my phone. They get attracted to the light. Everyone loves light. Nobody likes towns. Everybody wants to be here in Bombay. I saw the ugly creature crawling towards my phone, hopping over on to it, and then dancing on the screen. It became a little nightclub of that ugly rascal. Music, flashing lights, everything was there for him. He was dancing, and in the background, it continued: "Priyanka Calling."

I moved my face closer to the insect. I watched him closely. It stopped dancing. I looked at him. He looked at me. I saw his small eyes, small mouth, small anus. They are so much like us. No doubt they like lights like us.

'Hey you sister-fucker. Do you think I should answer her call,' I asked the insect. It moved his tentacles. 'Oh, I should. But how? See, till you are sitting on my phone and think that this is some discotheque of yours, I will not be able to talk to my girl. I have a solution.' It stopped moving its tentacles. 'I will have to kill you.'

"BAM!" Ugly creature was no more. Sometimes I felt if it was so easy to take your own life as well.

'Hey Priyanka, Was sup!' I answered the call, with the corpse of the dead insect still in my palm.

'Where the fuck have you been. I tried your number approximately hundred times.'

'Forgot the cell phone in the room. Was busy killing somebody. You say, how have you been.' I pulled out one of his tentacles.

'I am good. First tell me, what did you bring for me?' Time to get manipulative. Adding a tinge of romance is the best ingredient in the recipe of fooling girls.

'I am back. Isn't that a good enough gift for you.'

'Yes it is.' See, it worked. Ha! 'Listen, I have something important to tell you. Let's meet up.'

'Yeah! I also have something *very* important to tell you. For sure let's meet up.' I said and smashed the body of the dead insect. A sprinkle of fluorescent green fluid scattered on my palm. I hung up.

Out of all the positive things of being Priyanka's friend, the best was that she used to come and pick me up in her swashbuckling Black Toyota Corolla. Bombay looks so peaceful, so quiet, whilst observing it, sitting in an AC car. The moment you roll down the windows, it starts shouting. You pull it back up, it goes quiet again. Those tinted glasses create that mirage.

We sat in a cozy corner at Salt Water grills in Bandra.

'So, what was the important thing you wanted to tell me?'

'I want you to come with me on a trip to Lonavala.' Now I was in no mood to go anywhere with her and her gang of girls and few other shaved rascals.

'Only me and you. On a bike.' Now that came as a pleasant surprise. A kind of surprise which was not coming my way since long. I played it cool.

'Ah! I had just taken a leave from work. They won't allow me anymore days.'

'Oh come on. Who cares for a call center job. And anyways, it's just a matter of four days. You can give them any damn excuse. They will buy it. I know you are good at that.' Definitely I am *very* good at that. 'And even if they kick you out, there are thousands of call centers in this city. You can show them your middle finger and hop on to some another company. At both the places you have to be abused by the Americans, so why fret over this.' She was sounding so right. But why is she adamant that I should come with her. I became a bit curious. Who knows, may be some pundit is waiting in Lonavala. May be she is also planning a discreet marriage.

'Why this sudden plan?'

'It's not sudden. I wanted to go on a road trip across the country, but it never looked like it will happen. Earlier parents never approved of the idea because of my slight limping problem, later I never got a chance. So why not now.'

'And why Lonavala?' I asked and came up with my own answer in my head, "Because I have a pundit hidden behind some bushes over there who will tie us by the sacred thread of marriage."

'Have you ever been to Lonavala?'

'No!'

'Then come with me, and see for yourself how beautiful it is.' I told her that I will let her know by evening.

That was to buy time. Actually I wanted to double-check if there was enough money in my bank account. When I did so, I was again pleasantly surprised. I had returned in a general compartment, thus saving some money, plus the new month's salary had just been credited. One of the privileges of being on a paid leave, which I will not be getting this time as I will be bunking for Priyanka's sake. I thought I also need to freshen up a bit. To forget that Zareen drama that had unfolded a few days back.

I called up Priyanka and told her that I am all set.

Now how contrasting are the lives of the two girls in my life. The town one is so complex, the city one is ultra cool. One can't wear anything except the veil. One can wear anything under the sun, right from mini shorts, to bikinis, or even roam around naked if she wants. One can't step out without permission, other can go out of the milky-way galaxy without much of a hassle. One is so religious, other doesn't know a jack of religion.

It's such a pain in the ass to fall in love with a town girl. They stick to you. Whilst a city girl may go around with you for a week, a month or a year, and then when you hump them and then dump them, they simply move on. They don't sit back and wait for you. They will not shed a bucket of tears or swear that they will commit suicide, or break their bangles in that melodramatic fashion if you leave them. They are not rigid. They are so free. *Open minded* as they say.

My advise-: Always have an affair with a city babe. May be marry a town girl. Ha!

We hired a bike and were soon on the roads. On our way to Lonavala. She was wearing a long loose T-shirt, almost knee length, like those rappers wear. And grey slacks, with a small rucksack on her back, sunglasses and a huge smile on her face.

Our bike zipped across smoothly, leaving the city rush way behind us and we now were on the Pune-Mumbai expressway. The weather kept getting better. The serene, pure breeze ripped my face from the fore while Priyanka on the pillion, held me tight. We stopped many a times on our way. Once to eat hard candy sweet *chikki*, once because she just wanted to stand on a highway and look at the cars and trucks cruising by, once because it started to drizzle and we needed some shelter, and once because I needed to pee. She was genuinely looking happy and her smile was not crafty. She was enjoying every bit of it.

Our bike was cruising along a dense forest on the sides. It was quite dark now, but still enough light to see her smiling face in the rear mirror. The density of the forest thinned, and we figured out something.

'Hey look. There is a lake out there.' Priyanka announced. I parked the bike and we ran towards the water. Not stopping or daunted by the strong pointed barks of trees or the crickets and frogs making nasty sounds. Gasping, panting we ran into the lake and into each other's arms. Our clothes all soaked up. Dripping wet. Her long white shirt translucent now, good enough to reveal the contrasting black bra inside. She splashed some water on my face, I repeatedly on her breasts. Any part may go dry soon, I don't care, but not that.

When we finally came to a halt, we noticed that a boy of around seven years was shooting us with a plastic gun of his. "Dhishkaon! Dhishkaon!" We turned our heads and realized that a whole family of around 20 members was looking at us, sitting on a wicker mat around 50 meters away. Probably what they call, a family picnic of sorts was going on. Priyanka held me, peeped over my shoulder. There was a cake in the center of the house, with candles poked on its face.

'Let's go a little farther. Away from this kid before he shoots us dead.' She dig her fingers in my arms as we walked.

'Why haven't they flamed up the candles? What's the use of a candle if not illuminated?' I snapped.

'I don't know if you know of many uses, but I know some more uses of a candle.' She looked into my eyes, deep, 'even when they are not illuminated.' I gave her a perplexed look. She pulled her fingers out from my arm, and stood facing me. Her hair strands rough and wet, her face covered with small droplets of water. She thumped me slightly on the chest and kept pushing me back.

'See, I will explain through a real story. *One of my friends used to study in a boarding school. She said that her school mess daily provided them with a banana. One full banana. One day suddenly the mess started giving them bananas chopped into as many pieces as possible.*' She stopped pushing me with that.

'*When the girls questioned, they were told that a full banana was being used for more.*' A grin embellished her face. 'Now did you understand the uses of a candle and a banana my dear Ameen Jalal. Or do you need some more examples to understand.' I was too bemused, jumbled and nervous to give an answer.

She moved a good five feet away from me. And then removed her grey slacks. I was all wet, but my throat went dry. She pulled down her panties. I looked down. I turned back to make sure that the family is at a good distance. They looked as small as cars on the ground from the 21st floor. When I turned around to Priyanka, she had placed her fingers between her legs. Her wet, knee length t-shirt the only barricade now. She kept the entrance safe with her hands stretching the shirt way down her knees. She moved towards me. I was transfixed. Numb. I kept looking at the ground, then just at her beautiful feet, and then moving up to her lips, her eyes and finally the whole woman.

She stopped right in front of me. Turned around, and bent in front of me. Left the shirt loose, and offered herself to be swallowed all. By now my desire for her had transcended my powers to think or listen or speak or see or smell. I was all gone. I pounced on her fundaments like a hungry tiger, bit them apart and dipped my tongue in her wetness. She moaned and smiled and it looked like the sun has just risen again and its morning, afternoon, evening, night, all at the same time.

I moved my hands everywhere. She moved her lips everywhere. She began work on my lips, probing gently drawing me towards her. Her skin soft and slippery now. She was naked now, but her sunglasses were still on. I needed to look into her eyes for support. I snatched the glasses off her face. Her seducing eyes looking more beautiful and sexier than ever before.

Then we were almost into each other. I moved, she moved and we moved. Our slow rhythm gave way to urgent and demanding thrusts of passion. Doing it like two crazy dopers. My cocaine was her body and her hashish was my body. With all the strength of my blows, I left her in oblivion again and again.

Soon our bodies were wet because of the lake's water and soon wet for so many other reasons. Finally we were not giving company to the crickets and frogs in making any noises. Just lying there, far away sun dipping in the lake, the day ready to sleep. Her thighs over mine, my hands over her flat stomach, playing with her navel. Looking at the sky. Poker faced.

'Did we just now do something correct? Will you regret it?' I asked.

Love, Lust & Lies

'Will you?' She wore her glasses once again. I thought, she probably wasn't very happy.

'I don't think we did something morally right?'

She turned her face towards me, 'see, the bitterest tears shed over graves are for words left unsaid and deeds left undone. We haven't done anything wrong.' I noticed some crows flying over us, heading back to their nests.

'The crows were watching us. Must be saying, shameful jerks.' We broke into a small guffaw.

'Let them watch. Let them learn a few things from us. I swear they will be thankful.' She smiled again and sun rose again. She kissed me as deep as all the oceans and all the seas and all the lakes, rivers, ravines and oases put together. She pulled up her thighs, stuck between mine and placed it at the place where it matters the most. I was all set to pounce on her once again. We rolled and rolled and rolled and rolled.........

On that serene, usually quiet banks of that lake, in that hustle bustle of our two bodies, when I was in her and she was in me, I remember she had moaned, "I love you Ameen. I love you." ·

Bang! Bang!
Aah! Aah!
Bang! Bang!
Aah! Aah!

Sex was nothing new for us now. No more novice, we were veterans soon. Things which interest you, you pick them up quick. We picked it up real quick. Initially, the sessions used to end quickly. But with time we mastered the art. Enjoying each other to the core. We had done it with clothes on, and fully naked, letting each other worship each other's body. We had done it in every other possible way. She on top, me on top, rolled up, curled up, standing, and sitting. Name it. We had done it.

We had done it in every possible place. In her bedroom, in her balcony, on the couch, in the kitchen, in the lift, in the bathtub, in her car and even in that ramshackle which was our little smoking hub. In order to pay tribute to the game of basketball, she wanted to rub against me on a basketball court on a moonless night. I rubbished the idea though. More than thrilling, it sounded scary. There were lots and lots of risks involved. Especially of the Gurkha. They are very good at observing things, and who won't notice *such* a thing.

One day after we had rubbed against each other, I spotted a newspaper lying in her room. I flipped it open to know what's making news. Priyanka got irate at that.

'Why do you go back to the newspapers. Can't we talk a little. Come here. Lie down.' She would pull me back on her pillow, twirl my hair strands, check my cheeks to make sure that I was shaving regularly, kiss me for no reason, introduce me to her fat teddy a dozen times, tell me to say hi to him, tell the teddy to say hi to me, then ask the teddy if he likes me, then ask me if I like the teddy, then tell the teddy to kiss me, then tell me to kiss the teddy, and then we both would kiss the teddy together.

Is that enough or shall I narrate some more of my experiences with the teddy to tell you how irritating that fat furry jackass was. INSANE!

'Why do you read the newspapers?' She asked.

'To keep myself updated about activities in the world.'

'Am I not your world. Keep yourself updated on me.' Now I tell you, these rich kids have no respect for things like newspapers, books and magazines. At the most in the mornings while having their glass of juice in one hand, TV running full blast in their faces, legs perched on their sofas, they would flip the pages hurriedly as if the paper is giving electric shocks to them. Only those magazines they would earnestly read in which nothing but crap is printed, like, "ten things you must know about men." "Hundred things women love in bed." "Ask Dr. Kamini about your sex problems." "Are you satisfied with your sex life." And other such assorted stuff.

But I am not like that. I know the importance of these books and newspapers. I have seen kids giving exams without their course books, borrowing or stealing so that they can study some. Over here, they buy the books their college professor advice, they buy the books their personal tutor advice, they buy the books their friend advice and then keep it on their shelves to show it off. Hardly ever they open it. The day exams get over, they trash it in the bin.

The poor kid doesn't. He keeps it safely with him. At the end of the year, he takes the whole set and resells them to second hand buyers so that he can have enough money to buy the books for next year.

'So what are the newspapers telling you these days?' She asked.

'That Pratibha Patil is our new president. And also about protests over Bangladeshi feminist writer Taslima Nasreen turned violent. A few days back they also talked about Bismillah Khan, the legendary Shehnai player who passed away.'

'No stupid! Everyone knows about these things. Tell me something scandalous that has happened. Tell me something which I missed while flipping the newspaper.'

'Okay! Let me think.' I looked at the ceiling fan going round and round, squinted my eyes, thinking.

'A rich beautiful girl wanted to marry a guy of his own choice. But because the boy belonged to a different caste, her parents didn't approve of their marriage. So she, along with her boyfriend, chopped her parents into small-small pieces and threw them in the sea, and ran away to live happily ever after.'

Pin drop silence in the room for a minute. I thought she got scared. I continued, 'But guess what? They still didn't end up living happily ever after. She later found out that the guy was cheating on her, so she chopped him as well into small-small pieces. And now police nabbed her day before yesterday.' I turned to her, 'I am sure you skipped this news.'

'No I didn't.' She gave a half smile. 'I know about this one. This is too scandalous to give a miss.' The silent room came to life again when somebody knocked on the door.

'Daddy is here. He wants to meet you.' Mrs. Khanna said. I had heard about her father being at home after quite a long time.

'My god! Look who is here. My father. Can you believe that? He found some time out for me. Wait, I will be back in a jiffy.' She walked out. I went out in her balcony and Gazed at this wild city. Shimmering, glowing. And then I heard the *muezzin's* voice. Coming out from some loudspeaker attached to the minaret of some mosque out there. Calling all the believers to the home of the lord. I had not been to a mosque since so long. God was calling me. I had no time for him. I snooped back inside and plugged in the earphones of her I-pod. Another of mankind's greatest discoveries. It makes sure that you listen to things that you exactly want to listen.

There were songs by Led Zeppelin, Akon, Anastasia, Celine Dion, Shakira, Britney Spears, Avril Lavigne. There was no Indian name in there. No Lata, no Asha, no Alka. Americans are influencing our young children way too much. I guess the day is not far when one of these kids will run up his terrace, pull down the tricolor and unfurl the starry banner. And then the struggle to attain freedom will start all over again. A Gandhi, a Bose, a Maulana Azad will again be needed. Chances are negligible that people like these will come again, forcing us to be servants for another 500 years.

Moments later the door swung open and stormed in Priyanka, face flushing with anger, red. Slammed the door close. I immediately dropped the I-pod. She turned to me, furious.

'Tell me one thing. Will you chop my parents into small-small pieces and throw them in the sea.' I kept staring her, trying hard to make sure that I don't squeak.

'No, I won't.' Confused. She didn't expect me to say that, even as a joke. 'Because later, *you* will chop me into pieces.' Her anger flushed out a bit. Her red face turned pink, and then she hugged me. I ran my hands over her cheeks and they turned white again.

With sex, I officially became her boyfriend. And after a round of exams that summers, we both were graduates. I had come out way too rich than other students. Money, girlfriend, and degree, I had it all. Now that is what you call progress. I was still in Bombay for many obvious reasons. I was still working at a call center, looking for an admission in a business school and of course Priyanka's curves were always on my mind.

We got along like a house on fire. Our relationship kept on getting stronger and stronger. And as I was spending more time in her house than ever before, I noticed that the relationship between Priyanka and her parents was not very cordial. There were cracks galore. But to be honest, I was not surprised to find that out. In metros, parents are hardly finding time for their kids, kids are spending way too much time outside doping and watching porn with their friends. Things such as these were bound to happen. This is another disease we are being infected with. The concept of nuclear family is overtaking the old formulae of joint family. Earlier the words "My Family" meant my parents, my siblings, my grandparents, my uncle-aunties, my nephews, my cousins, my cousin's-cousins and many more. It was one big Indian family. But now "My Family" means me, my teddy, my dog, my car, my cell phone, my laptop, my new hot girlfriend and my I-pod. We are loving things and using people, this is the reason for so much hatred all around. It got to be other way round. Loving people and using things.

While sneaking out that day I saw her father drinking in front of the TV, his big belly loaded with alcohol, a thick gold chain around his neck, sitting in a white pajama, bare chest. He was looking like an ogre, a yeti. I quietly stepped out.

Life for me was going fine. I was making money at nights, screwing Priyanka in mornings, and going around in her car in the evenings. Till that gruesome day when Haider fell ill. He had high fever. I told him to visit a doctor. He refused, taking it lightly. It was not to be taken lightly because with passing days his condition deteriorated big time. Soon he complained of severe headache, muscle and joint pains. Bright red rashes appeared first on the lower limbs and the chest; and then covered most of his body. He had dengue. A fatal disease responsible for taking lives of many of my countrymen. I rushed him to the hospital and got him admitted. But we knew that we had come in late. Lying on his folding he said, 'Ameen, can you read my horoscope. I want to know when will I get well.' I got the newspaper and read it out.

'It's going to be a healthy month for you.' I threw the newspaper back.

Haider smiled and said, 'you remember what I told you about how this thing works. On the contrary. I am going to be dead soon.' I gagged him and told him to shut up.

'You are going nowhere. These horoscopes are all bullshit.' But I was scared of losing my friend. I again visited the mosque and promised once again that I will get my beard back. I prayed five times a day, I kept fasts. But guess what? He died. We buried him in a graveyard in Bandra. All autumn I sat near his grave, crying and weeping and clearing the fallen leaves from the paunch of his grave. I was never going to see Haider again.

And with that the city again started looking hostile to me. I no more liked its pace, its speed. I wanted to go back to my town. To be with Zareen. At times when I thought of Zareen, a fear would grip me. How must she be right now. Do her parents know about us. Do my parents know about us. The coward in me would tell me to stay back. To think of something else, but would fail. The call center and the night shifts would then torture me. American's abuses started sounding like abuses.

To be honest, the inside story of those glasses and majestic steel buildings is something else. Nothing looks hunky-dory after a while. After all, till when can one keep his eyes open at night like an owl in front of a computer. Till when can one sustain somebody shrieking in your ears through those headsets. It starts irritating you. Frustration, irritation grips you. Haider's demise was also not helping me. Going back to my room, sleeping alone used to bug me. Let me tell you the truth of these call center executives. Though they made movies and wrote books on call centers, they got it all wrong there. It's not the truth.

Honestly, every agent wants to break free of this world. Agreed, there is easy money and easy girls, but I can bet no one wants to stay for long. Nobody wants to make a career out there. It's like a makeshift tent for everybody. Part time. Like a whore. Fuck her, leave her. But over here, the whore pays you.

I am out of job. I am out of degree, I am out of money. Cool, you know English, jump in the band wagon. You ask anybody, and if he is honest, he will say that yes, I want to get out of this world. This world of headsets and computers and night shifts and American's abuses, cigarettes, drugs, etc. I had decided to quit this fucking world.

That night, my room was again haunting me. I desperately wanted company. And company now meant Priyanka. Luck was on my side as minutes later she called me up, saying that she wants to talk to me about something, urgently. I could make out from her voice that she had fought with her parents once again. I left for her house. Called her up from the lift and she discreetly unlocked the door.

Soon we ripped open each other, smashed each other, scratched each other and threw out on each other. All the time our fingers were in each other's mouth so that the noise doesn't go out of the four walls of her room. After a rough round of making out, we were lying in each other's arms.

'I don't like this city anymore. At times, I want to brake free and run away giving it all up,' she said.

186   Love, Lust & Lies

'So do I.' I accorded with her statement.

'My parents are trying to suffocate me to death. They won't allow me to go anywhere out of this dirty city. You tell me, am I still a toddler. They pamper me as if I don't know a jack-shit of this world. Why don't they wrap up a nappy around my ass, if I am still such a small child of theirs.' I lay there listening to her grievances. Pleased that she was at least not gibbering about her teddy.

'You know what these western kids do if their parents don't let them live their lives as they wish to. They sue them, drag them to court. Sometimes I feel to do the same.' See, that American influence again. 'Let's go and live somewhere else. Away from this dirty city, dirty people. What do you say?' Till now everything was sounding immature to me. Priyanka blabbering and venting her frustration on her family by bad mouthing them was nothing new to my ears. But there was something more to it today. Her tempo, her exasperation, was all now at the upper range of her patience limit. She was sounding too flappable. Sounding a tad too serious.

'I want to see the world. There are so many places to be visited. So many Lonavalas to be discovered. But I can't go. In fact I have hardly been on a vacation before.' Now that was sad. Even my orthodox middle class parents would take me for a vacation annually.

'Why? Because they feel that your leg is still a problem.'

'No! Because I am not my father's daughter. I am somebody else's daughter who screwed my mom and ran away never to return.' That came as a shocker. Numb, I went on to listen the whole story.

'Dad was in the army, posted somewhere in the hills of Kashmir for about a year and a half. In the same phase, mom had an affair with some man. When she got pregnant with me, that son of a bitch dumped mom and returned never again. And the result was this illegitimate daughter of hers. Sometimes I feel why didn't she abort me then. She could have cried for a while with my foetus in her hands and it would have been all over.' A few tears rolled down the sides of her eyes. 'When dad returned, she pleaded guilty. Surprisingly, he forgave. Just to punish her and me all our lives. I am fed up Ameen. I am fed up.' She curled into me. Broke down. I tapped her forehead, caressed her palm.

That day I realized that lives in those titanic buildings, in those mesmerizing apartments is not so rosy as it seems. Rich people lead such horrendous lives. Such reprehensible lives. A poor man everyday fights for basic necessities of life. But his list of problems ends with that. Food, clothe and shelter is all they need and want. While these rich, they have everything. But they end up falling in chasms which are full of some unusual, disgraceful and shameful problems. For the first time I felt bad for the rich and happy to be born a poor.

'Take me away from this dirty town and dirty people Ameen.' I was still not sure what to say.

I burst out, 'where will we go? What will we do? It's not as easy as it sounds. Running away is not a good idea.'

'No. I don't know. I want you and me out of this place. We can live anywhere. I beg you. We are graduates now. We can find a job. Please Ameen. I want to be free. Can't you do this bit for me?' I stayed shut. And my silence pissed her off.

She stormed out of bed and blasted full on, 'don't act like a coward you bozo. You behave like an animal in that bed and when it comes to matters which matter, your manhood goes to sleep.' I had to get up and gag her to make sure she shuts up before her growling attracts her parents. She kept on throwing her head around, I kept on gagging her mouth, she pushed me hard on the wall, I gagged her, she pulled my hair, I gagged her, she was going nuts, I was going nuts gagging her. Finally she calmed down. Cried, and sat down on her bed.

I ignited a cigarette for both of us. She was still in tears, smoking and crying at the same time.

'Will you run away with me?' Now this time I didn't have an option of staying shut. Nor I could afford to say a no. She had got me in a spot.

'Okay, let's suppose we run away. What will we do. Do you have any idea how difficult it is to survive without a penny in your wallet and job in your hand.'

'I have a friend who writes for a magazine. They need freelance writers. I can write and mail them and get my payment regularly. Plus I have full confidence in you. You will find something for yourself.' Well, now that was flattering. She was quite intelligent.

'Where will we go?'

'Anywhere. Anywhere in this world. Take me anywhere with you, but here.' I had a place in mind. I didn't tell her right then. There were still many things which had to be taken care of. As for the moment I played it as cool as a level-headed buyer.

'What about my call center job?'

'Oh spit on it. You can do so much better. Just look at you. What it has done. Call centers have made a nocturnal fool out of you. And just the other day you were planning to quit this sick job.' She was right. I was hating it big time.

'So you have made up your mind that you will run away no matter what,' I asked again and again, hoping, she may change her mind.

'I have made up my mind that I will run away *with you*.' She pulled me closer to her. 'What will I do without you baby. It's about me and you and not about me and me. We will go around, fuck around, explore different places and as they say in fairy tales, live happy ever after.'

The problem with fairy tales is that they happen in fairy lands and not in dirty places where the most cunning creatures, human beings live. She was going mad with her ideas of running away. The only option I had now was to dump this stupid girl and run away somewhere else. Never to return. As the man in Mrs. Khanna's life did.

But No! I was not going to do that. I had failed to get ammi her freedom and she all her life remained under the darkness of her veil. I had failed to get Zareen with myself even after marrying her because of my cowardliness. I was not going to be a failure again. *I will go with her, wherever she wants to go. I am not going to dump her here so that she can be tortured by her old man. I will take her away. I will run along.*

'Will you love me the same way if I keep a beard?' I asked.

'Of course I will.'

'Will you be ashamed of going for a movie with me in a kurta pajama and beads in my hand?'

'Not at all.'

'Will you not be scared of living with a mullah?'

'Till you are not scared of walking on a beach with a babe in a bikini.'

'Why should I be. Let the world see, how beautiful my love is.'

'People will gossip.'

'Let them gossip. Let them learn a few things from us. Let the world see and be amazed to see a mullah and a babe together.'

To make me believe that we will be doing the right thing, she gushed, "Sometimes you just have to close your eyes and leap off the precipice, unmoved by the daunting growls of the rabid dog named fear."

'Wow! Which great writer wrote these great lines?'

'I made it.'

'No, you didn't. You liar.'

'Yes I did.'

"No, you didn't. I have seen that movie. The writer is Larry Doyle and not you, miss Priyanka Khanna'

'Make it Priyanka Jalal. Sounds better.'

And we laughed and we kissed again, tore open each other and rolled all over each other once again. I eat life out of her, and she sucking life out of me.

I think I was turning into a communist. A follower of Marxism and Leninism. And I feel every communist that ever walked this planet became one once he realized that this world is absolutely stinking with so much of poverty and disparity. Once he is forced to realize the value of every rupee in his wallet. When he realizes that he is being robbed of something, or the state is being unfair to him. When he realizes that the rich and the poor should be at par. When he decides, enough is enough, let's slay these rich. I think this world badly needs a Robin-hood and his band of merry men who used to rob the rich, and help the poor.

I don't feel that the rich or the capitalists give enough importance to a one rupee coin, except for times when they need a change. And I say that in reference to the rich kids mostly, and not their parents. See, most of the so called rich people in Bombay came here like me, from small towns and villages, with a rag and a few wad of notes. They worked hard and made money. They changed sides. They became rich. But their kids. Those horrible kids. They got it all very easy. Money, clothes, watches, cars, AC, education, girls, everything. When you get something that easy, you don't value it. Like we have forgotten the importance of our own freedom. We think it's our birth right. They started feeling that being rich is their birth right.

But when you really run out of money, and you have to eat and drink, and travel and survive on a mere sum of fifty rupees a day, that one rupee coin looks so very important. You count and save every penny that you are left with.

We had decided to quit this city. But we still didn't know how we were going to do it. No plans at all. It would all be like running in a dark tunnel towards that small glimpse of light at the other end, hoping that it doesn't turn out to be a train that will run us down. Apart from anything else, what we needed the most was money. A good and hefty sum to make a fresh beginning.

I and Priyanka never talked about it as there were chances that we may use it as an excuse and call off all our plans. I was saving every possible nickel and dime, but how much can one save by saving only in nickels and dimes. I needed more. We needed more.

We had decided to run on the 1st of January. "A new year, a new beginning," was our tagline. A few days were left for the D-day to arrive, but still no luck. I was not finding any solution. Chances were getting thinner and thinner with every passing day. Mood always grim whenever I thought about it. "How to be rich? How to be rich? How to be rich?" Was all I dwelling upon. Call center savings would run out quick and fast. How to get that extra cash? I knew I was not lucky enough to win a lottery, not brave enough to rob a bank, not intelligent enough to win a "Kaun Banega Crorepati." Not even smarter than a fifth grader to win a million rupees. There was nothing enough in me to make me rich enough.

Sitting at the Marine Lines promenade, eating a sweet-corn for my dinner, watching the waves splash harshly against the walls, I was hoping to draw some inspiration. Some idea. Some way to make it big. This sea has been there for ages. It saw Adam and Eve. Alexander and Napoleon. Harappans and the Mughals. British and Portuguese. Gandhi and Nehru. It knew so much. May be the wise sea will tell me a trick. So I sat there, and sat there whole night.

A million cars passing by thinned in numbers to thousands, to hundreds, to a time when a couple of cars would pass by every ten minutes, full with bunch of wild party animals. Playing music all aloud, cigarettes between their lips, bottles of the costliest champagne in their hands and hottest girls in their laps. Why didn't God give me a rich father like them? Why was I to be born in a middle class family? Why was I to play this part of a wretched man called Ameen Jalal?

Soon it was me, waves, streetlights, and a few men with broom sticks cleaning and clearing the garbage thrown away by some very responsible citizens of our country. A few people were working on a huge hoarding, changing the poster on display. A smiling woman's face was replaced by a dog's face. That dog was of more worth than me. And they say it's a dog's life. Huh!

A few massagers with their small kits came into scene. They thump your head and relax you in every possible way just for a mere sum of ten rupees. I summoned one and he poured some coconut oil on my head and started giving me a *champi* - a head massage with his strong hands.

He was hammering my head, "Dhug, Dhug, Dhug, Dhug, Dhug, Dhug." The streetlights were bouncing with my head. The cars with those rascals passing in a woozy flash. A few prostitutes came over, called me, and went away. I saw Haider in a flash, in slo-mo saying, "They are eunuchs Ameen. They are eunuchs. Don't go to them. You will go inside to screw them, come back screwed instead." And then he laughed hysterically. And then he went away. And then came Pinocchio with his son, the nose-pecker, and his wife Khurshid. Nose-pecker digging for gold in his nose, Khurshid showing off her big nose ring, and then Pinocchio came right into my face and said, "How did you find Bombay Ameen. Did you like the tall buildings and fast roads. Isn't the city organized Ameen." And then he came closer and announced to the whole world, "You rotten son of a villager, I made a fool out of you, and see how easily I ruined your life by getting you out of your peaceful land into this sinful world." And then he laughed hysterically. And then they all came back. They all laughed hysterically. Haider, prostitutes, all the urchins that served me at small restaurants, the imam of the mosque, cigarette vendor, ticket-checker, dwarf, Mr. Gupta, Zain, Sheezan, Rohan. They all came and they all laughed hysterically and shouted, "You rotten son of a villager." They all laughed at my apathy, at my miserable condition, at my biggest mistake of falling in love with Priyanka, at my shamelessness for duping Zareen.

And then I saw Zareen and Priyanka as well. But standing on the other side. Crying. *Crying with me. Crying for me.*

Suddenly somebody poked me with a stick and I opened my eyes with a jolt. I had fallen asleep on the promenade itself. The sun was still not out, but the color of the sky was turning light black, indicating that the sun was on its way. It was that hour in which the drivers of the cars are a bit confused. Half of them drive with their headlights on, while half of them keep them off. It's neither morning, nor night. It's somewhere in between. People had started with their rounds of morning walks while newsvendors were on their jobs with stacks of newspapers riding the pillion of their bicycles.

It was a bald old man, with a thick glass, with a stoop poking me still with his stick.

'Get up young man.' I opened my eyes, but he kept on poking me. Seemed he also wanted to extract some fun of my miserable condition. 'You look from a good family. That's why I tell my grandchildren not to drink...'

'Will you stop poking me that stick of yours you bald old rotten man.' He immediately pulled his stick back. I realized he was just trying to help.

'I am sorry for that.' I apologized.

'Don't worry. It happens. Did you dream something bad?'

'Very bad indeed.'

That morning sun rose for one last time in that particular year. Tomorrow when this fireball goes up in the sky, the dates would have rolled, calendars changed. And hopefully my life too. I had to do something today. I had this one day. I had seen some old relatives of mine in that dream. Actually my only relatives in Bombay, Pinocchio and his family. Probably he became my last hope. I was all set to go and beg and borrow, or even steal money from him.

It was the New Year Eve. And a new year is welcomed with a lot of pomp and splendor in Bombay. They drink and dance and dope and hump girls that evening. But I had no such plans for that night. I was on a different mission. A mission that could help me start a new life in the coming year. Last time I visited Pinocchio's place was actually my first day in Bombay. And ironically, today is the last day in this city. No doubt they say, "what goes around, comes around."

When I reached Pinocchio's residence, he was not at home. Khurshid answered my knock on the door. She peeped out.

'Look who is here. Ameen Jalal.' She said with a sarcasm that had been with her since she was in her mother's paunch. I walked in. Nose-pecker was there on the sofa, picking nose. Sometimes I wish I can light a torch and look inside his two caves of nose how much stuff is in there that it never gets over. God blesses some people with some things in plenty.

'So what suddenly reminded you of us?'

'Today is my last day in Bombay. Thought that I should thank you for what all you guys have done for me.' That was to lick her ass before I hammer it hard.

'We changed your life. Isn't it?'

'Yeah! I owe you a lot.'

'But your college got over way back. What are you doing in Bombay since then.'

'I was working in a call center.'

'Hmm, making lots of moolah.' It was then that she offered me a chair to sit and water to drink. 'So, going back home with your earnings now.' It was time to hammer her ass.

'No! I want some money as a loan from you guys. I will return it very soon.'

'Why do you need money? Didn't you make enough of it at those call centers. Or wasted it all on girls and liquor.'

'No!'

'Then why?'

'I am running away with a girl.' She looked at nose-pecker with an open mouth. Nose-pecker looked back with an open mouth.

'Hindu girl?' I nodded.

'Rich girl?' I nodded.

'Rehan, get sweets for the boy. Must be hungry *na*. Is she the only daughter of her father?'

I nodded yet again. Nose-pecker's mouth refusing to collapse.

'Is he giving lots in dowry.' I didn't nod this time.

'I said I am running away with her. Not marrying her.' She pushed the chair with her leg I was about to place my tired ass on.

'Rehan, cancel the sweets. I thought a call center executive had come to our house. But it turned out to be a beggar. We don't have any money-*shoney* to waste on fools like you who fall in love without caring for their parents or religion. The first day I saw you, I knew you will turn out to be a big headache for your old father. You shameless moron, do you know how big a sin it is to marry a Hindu girl. Have you gone nuts?'

She kept on blasting me. I quietly stood there with a sad, loser's expression on my face. To be honest, it didn't matter. I had been abused so many time that it all went in one ear and came out of another. It had become a habit.

Minutes later, in walked Pinocchio, giving a new lease to my dying hope. He was from that old school of thought, where one values relations and respects needs of other people. He came from a small town to Bombay like me. He will *help* me for sure, I thought.

'See, your relative just turned into a vagabond. He is begging us to give him some money.'

'Why? What happened Ameen?' Pinocchio asked, I fell straight on his legs.

'I will tell you. This loafer wants money so that he can run away with a girl he claims to be in love with.' That was Khurshid. Pinocchio held my shoulders to get me up.

'A Hindu girl. Without letting Muqarram or Najma know. Secretly.' Pinocchio left me, letting me fall once again.

'Uncle, please help me. I need it badly. You guys are my last hope. I swear to return it very soon.'

'*Oh ho!* And where will you get it from. Will your girl dance at bars and sleep at brothels.'

Pinocchio went inside his room. That was enough. My last hope had just then shattered. I had tried to borrow enough, I had begged enough. There was only one final way left in front of me. I had already set my eyes on something.

I continued weeping. Then said, 'okay, I don't want any money. But can I at least sleep here tonight. I have already left my room and my luggage is at a friend's place. I will be leaving tomorrow. First train.' That wretched lady still had problems.

'No, you can't. Our house is already full, and there is no space. Check a hotel.' Now walking out of that room would have

Love, Lust & Lies

made things hell lot of a difficult for my future. Luckily, Pinocchio shouted from inside, 'It's fine Khurshid. He can stay here. Can sleep with Rehan.' I thanked him. *I still had my chance.*

Now while the whole world celebrates New Year outside, some families still prefer to take a nap inside. They don't see anything glorious when the date turns 1st January. For them, it's just another day. Pinocchio's family was one of them. They didn't believe in dancing and doping while bringing the New Year in. Lights went out as usual at around ten. I lied down next to nose-pecker. Acting asleep in the dark.

After about two hours, I opened my eyes. Looked at the nose-pecker, waved my hands over his eyes. Asleep! I picked up a small duffel bag hanging on a nail on one of the walls of the room. I then walked towards Pinocchio's room. Softly! Making sure no one wakes up. There was another small room inside Pinocchio's room. My future was waiting for me in there.

I tip-toed inside that small room. And right in front of me, right in front of my eyes was his steel locker. A set of keys were right behind it. My heart was racing faster than the *khut-khut* of a fast local train. My hands were trembling more than a hundred year old lady's would. But my senses were all in place. I opened it, and bundles of money and jewelry smiled at me from inside. I didn't have time to smile back. In minutes, I had it all in my bag. I sneaked out of the room, as cautious as before. Opened the main door and ran for my life.

The sky was illuminated with a thousand crackers going mad. The clock had just struck twelve. Somebody right then would have kissed his girl, while somebody might have humped. Some would have just taken a sip of alcohol, while some drank the whole bottle neat. Some would have just taken a drag of weed, while some would have just sniffed. They were doing such small things in life. I had done the biggest and the most important of all. I had changed my life. Well, almost.

A drunkard bootlegger was lying in a corner, repeating, 'Happy new year. Happy new year. Happy new year.' Like those key toys rich children play with. You turn the key and leave the toy, and it would run and sing and dance monotonously. The bootlegger was doing something similar. I was rich now. I felt it's my responsibility to share some with him. Like a communist, I dropped a one rupee coin in his aluminum bowl. He looked up at me, smiled. Rich don't care for one rupee coins. Poor bootleggers do. He wished me Happy new year. I went close to him.

'No! It's happy new life. Happy new life Ameen. A very happy new life.' I exulted.

"The old skin has to be shed before the new one can come."

Joseph Campbell

I did shed it. Didn't I? I am a thief now.

Nevertheless, I was all set to go to Nainital. *We,* were all set to go to Nainital. And don't ask me, why I say, 'WE.'

Sometimes I feel that it's all written, *kismet,* as they say. Joining madrasa, then jumping to a school, coming to Bombay, meeting Priyanka, marrying Zareen and now going fugitive. It all looked planned for a moment and a coincidence the other moment. But why was I to make a thief out of myself in the end. Why was I to commit such a horrible act, just to be with the person I yearned to be with the most? The answer is again, *kismet.*

Somebody had said that true lovers don't look into each other's eyes, but in the same direction. Going by this, we were in true love. We were both looking at our new lives. She, with a huge smile and I, with a huge grin. We had taken a train from Chatrapati Shivaji Terminus for Hazrat Nizamuddin Station. We were heading from one mega city of this country to another. From Bombay to Delhi. From there, then we would take a bus to my old city, my Nainital. It was time to say *Hasta-La-Vista* Bombay. It taught me a lot, it made a man out of a boy, and a thief out of a man. I remember when I was leaving for Bombay, ammi had quipped, "you are going out a youngster, but I am sure you will come back a star." I was definitely a star now. A star *thief.*

Priyanka was happier than I had ever seen her before. She was flourishing, blossoming with joy. I was glad. Glad, that I was able to get one girl in my life free of the chains. Of the shackles. Of the hawsers. But it had all come at a cost. A cost I hadn't told her about. And would probably never tell her as well. I was a thief now. A thief on the run. Though I was not worried about the police at all. See, more than my fugitive skills, I was confident that the police will not be able to trace me. They just can't. *They are so good at their jobs you see.*

Just before taking train, I had called up abba and told him that I was leaving Bombay as I found some work in Kerala in a small hotel as a manager. That was to fool the police. If they somehow get active for a couple of days and try to trace me. They would call abba for sure. They would go all the way south to hunt me down, and I will be sitting pretty in the laps of Himalayas. Tired, they would give up soon. It's so easy to fool the Indian police. Ha!

And even if they do somehow manage to trace me, I should not be worried. I am rich now. I can make their fat ass a little more fat by digging in some bundles. Things will die down right there.

I kept on opening the bag, the most important of all the bags, every fifteen minutes to make sure that I was still rich. I had been poor for so long that it took a lot of time for this new tag to sink in. This *rich* tag.

Priyanka didn't sleep the whole journey. Like a kid, stuck to her window seat, enjoying every bit of her freedom. All she had carried was her laptop, her I-pod, her cyber shot, her teddy and a few clothes. When our train crossed a bridge, under which flew the majestic Tapti river, a few passengers threw coins through the window grills to impress the river god. Priyanka did the same. "For our future," she had quipped just before flinging it. "What a waste of a rupee," I thought. Nevertheless, I was happy as she was happy.

We kept on crossing villages and farmlands and rocks and boulders and cows and goats and poles and children selling water and children selling magazines. We crossed all of them and I was happy that we were crossing all of them real quick. Sooner the better.

We crossed Nagpur and we had oranges, we crossed Bhopal and we had *paan*, we crossed Gwalior and we saw the glowing Gwalior fort perched on a hill like the king eagle, looking majestic and more, we crossed Kanpur and I bought her a leather sandal, we crossed Lucknow and I told her about the so called *"pehle aap lucknowi tehzeeb"* which ironically no more exists.

She clicked our pictures every other second. While eating oranges, while wearing her sandals. And then transferred all the pictures to her laptop and gave all of them captions. "Me, Nagpur and my Orange." "Me, Kanpur and my Sandals." Some similar stupid captions. There was some strange satisfaction she used to achieve after doing all that nonsense stuff. But all that stupidity of hers used to turn me on big time. As it had all my college life.

At night, when the night bulbs were flickering in the whole compartment, and every soul was asleep, I pounced on her. As I had said, we were veterans now, such sex was necessary to keep the charm alive. She was scared that someone may catch us. My fingers gauged her depth, and she was never bothered again. With only the buttons and the zips of our jeans unlocked, and our bodies swinging in the old pendulum fashion, we did the needful on a train berth.

Early next morning, we entered the capital. We had left Bombay way behind, way far.

We moved out of the station and walked into one of the oldest cities in the world. Delhi. In winters this city gets too cold. It is one of those cities which are blessed with extreme type of climates. In summers the sun can burn your skin, while the winters can break your spine. Delhi is strategically placed between the Hindu Kush Mountains, Aravalis and the great Himalayan ranges. All the major hill stations surround Delhi. May it be Shimla, Kullu-Manali, Mount Abu, Musoorie. Making it extremely cold for various obvious reasons.

Being a north Indian, I had experienced such weather, but such chilling temperatures were absolutely new for a Bombayite. She started to shiver. I bought her an overcoat and a stylish golf cap to keep her warm. Roughly around midnight we boarded the bus for Nainital.

Those rickety state buses which jump more, ride less. Your ass is in pain every time it falls on seats less the cushion. But even those bumps were amusing us that night. Instead of cribbing, we were finding humor in all that. Being with your loved one probably does that. The bus was houseful. Families going on a vacation, and couples going for a romantic honeymoon filled most of the seats. We two were going on a honeymoon for a lifetime. When the journey started from Delhi, the bus was abuzz and alive, with families cracking jokes on each other, and kids running in the alley. But as we left Delhi behind, and Nainital inched closer, the night grew dark and cold and most of them were fast asleep. We were not. We had so many things to talk about.

And when we ran out of topics, we covered ourselves with a bed sheet, and the night remained beautiful, warm, and interesting. Outside, it was pitch dark, from the screen at the front of the bus all one could see were the two long streaks of the headlights. A little later Priyanka was fast asleep on my right shoulder. She was holding the teddy tight. I didn't like it. "This teddy is going to be such a nosy cow," I thought. I swiftly snatched the fatso out of her grip, looked at the silly creature for a brief second, and then held it outside the window. The teddy begged, "Mercy my lord. Mercy!" I didn't show any. I dropped the fat furry jackass. The tyres of the state bus pressed him under their enormous weight. Teddy was dead. And all I was glad.

Plains gave way to the mountains, and country side pastures gave way to thick forests. Roads no more remained linear, but circular. They turned and turned, and our bus turned and turned with them. And when it had turned at least half a million times, I could see the *bulbuls* and mynas leaving their nests, and the Kumaoni women with wicker baskets on their backs climbing the hills. I had made out that we had entered the paradise city of Nainital sitting majestically at the Kumaon foothills. After a few more sharp turns the bus came to a halt.

I climbed out of the bus and ran my eyes all around the paradise city. I saw Naina peak on the north, Deopatha on the west, and Ayarpatha on the south. It was still misty, a bit hazy, but good enough to see.

Our first aim was to buy a small house, somewhere around trees and bulbuls and mynas and a little away from the hustle bustle of tourists. A house just enough for two people to get cozy and fulfill their never ending desire for each other. For the time being we decided to take a room in a hotel. It was quite long now since we saw each-other as we wanted to. We quickly checked into a room, and slam banged the room door behind us. Cool breeze was flowing in from the open window. I pushed her back on the same door. Held her face in my palms,

'Welcome to Nainital.' I grabbed her lips in my pout. Held her tight and dug my nails deep into her fundaments. Our eyes met for a brief second and pleaded for a chance. Heated tongues met in the middle, our clothes found place on the floor one by one and skin got interlocked with skin. I drank her nectar and she my sap.

For the next few days our schedule remained very much the same.

Morning session of lazy love making. Breakfast not in a restaurant, but in our room as we fed each other. Then get into the bathroom together, come out after scrubbing each other real hard. Then fierce session of afternoon love making. And then strolling around Nainital the whole evening.

I used to take her around Nainital as a personal guide. Make her see different places and tell her my childhood stories. We kept mooching around for several days. Shot some balloons with air gun, did some horse riding, pedaled the boat across the eponymous lake several times. Went around the Tibetan market and Bara Bazaar. Checked out Jim Corbett's old residence and visited an old Christian graveyard which was full of tombs of British soldiers who were laid down to rest may be a good 200 years back.

One evening we passed a tattoo parlor. She told me that she always wanted to get one done. I told her to go ahead. A dragon erupting a fireball was engraved on her lower back and an angel with arms wide open on her shoulder.

Soon our very own house came in. A wonderful small cottage as we had planned. On the Ayarpatha hill, in the midst of trees and birds and fog and mist. I loved that little domicile of ours. There were two small rooms in all. And all the times it smelled of soaked wood, soaked soil and of course of a soaked Priyanka. The size of the house never mattered to us. Nor were we much interested in a lot of amenities. We didn't care. Never gave a damn. Materialistic thoughts never crossed our minds. We had no furniture at all. Our living room was our amusement arcade. We slept on a mattress. We passed so many evenings sitting idly on the front steps, staring at the trees, *langurs,* lantana bushes and at each other. Many a nights we brought the mattresses out under a roofless sky, just gazing at the innumerous stars up there.

We were two people who could never get enough of each other living on a single mattress. We were either sleeping, or

Love, Lust & Lies

talking, or eating, or reading, or making love on the mattress or on the floor or outside in the mist.

Soon a radio came in. The only channel that played on it was the All India Radio. Ameen Sayani was long gone, and after him, there was no jockey who had nice voice. News that was read at the stroke of midnight sounded like a melancholy and not trustworthy. Though All India Radio did something nice. It made Priyanka a fan of Rafi, Mukesh, Manna Dey and Kishore. The Zeppelins and the Britneys were shown the way out of her laptop and I-pod.

At night, with either Rafi or Mukesh humming in the background, I would read out stories with her head resting on my matted chest. She would listen like a good student.

When we ran out of ideas and had used our imagination to the core to use our bodies as insanely as possible, we would watch some great sex movies on her laptop and fucked like those sluts and porn-stars. She observed that the female in such movies never ever took her sandals off, so we also tried it with her sandals on. It never made a difference. Can Hugh Hefner please stand up and explain why do they never take their sandals off? Huh!

Every night after I would roll down from her body, panting, screaming her name, leaving her soaked, she would lie down on the mattress, naked. And I would lie there next to her, naked. And we would talk till the sun rose again. Our mattress was strategically placed in such a fashion that the first rays of light would travel from the window to illuminate her skin. Charging me up all over again and we would roll over each other all over again. The whole scenery would vacillate with our bodies. Would smile and laugh, and giggle and hoot with us. Our little ramshackle became our little world.

If you ask me, those were undoubtedly the best days of my life. It can be compared with a montage shot of any Hindi film, in which they show the hero-heroine having a blissful time in a sequence of quick cuts with a song in the background. Running around, dancing around, feeding each other, hugging each other, but they never show hero-heroine kiss or have sex. The censor board won't allow. They think kids will learn *bad* things. *Hypocrites!* I have a suggestion for these censor guys. Just check the TV channel your young and restless sons and daughters watch at nights, alone discreetly. And better if it's a Friday or a Saturday. *The cable operator plays some great sex movies on Fridays and Saturdays. Ha!*

Sitting in this dungeon, dying, I hope to live these days once again up there. They say, heaven is a place where you get a chance to live with your loved one once again. I would like to live with my babe. A mullah with his babe.

It's true, and a sad fact, that all good things come to an end. They have to. It is law of the nature. Sex comes in. Goes out. Lust. The same. Life. The same.

After a while, sex and lust attain satiety. And when it does, you start thinking about many other things in your life which were evading your mind when you were so involved with someone's body. Months had passed and I had never bothered of thinking about anything else, but Priyanka and her curves and her hips and her depths. The day I realized that there was more than Priyanka, or rather, the day sex for me reached the state of satiety, the first thing or person I thought about was Zareen.

Beads of chill sweat and anxiousness formed on my forehead. Things moved in my stomach ferociously. I felt as if I was till now living in oblivion. An ignorant life. Ignorance is bliss, but only for the irresponsible. Or the coward. I was the coward. And that was exactly what I was doing. My coward part was stopping me from telling anything to Priyanka about Zareen, or going all the way to Zareen and tell her about Priyanka.

At least do something to get Zareen out of the illusion, the fantasy world she must be living in, dreaming that I will be coming on a white horse, princely dressed to run away with her.

That night it was raining heavily, and in that ramshackle cum heaven of ours I was stroking Priyanka heavily. Growling her name from the back of my throat. Suddenly something caught my attention. Her eyes. They were white as milk. My strokes became clumsy, I was losing grip, my hip movement lost rhythm, and I went out incomplete. Worried and surprised, she asked the reason for my exodus act. I kept quiet.

Her white eyes were the reason. I had never noticed the whiteness of her eyes before, and I was not used to such white eyes. Traveling in those trains in Bombay, and living on footpaths, I had always seen men with red eyes. Tired eyes. A poor man's eyes are always like that. Mine were no different. Red, bloodshot and tired. It reminded me of her family background and my family background.

She had started to write for a magazine and was earning as well. As far as I was concerned, all I was doing was eating on her money and feeding on her body. Insecurity crept in. It had for the first time crept in me that night. As they say, men will be men. It's not a manly thing to eat on your partner's earnings. A man needs to earn and a woman needs to cook. It's an old theory which must be put away to rest as quickly as possible. But I somewhat still believed in that. You know that orthodox in me will take hell lot of time to die. And as I said earlier, old habits die hard.

Similarly, my habit of grabbing a newspaper after playing with her body had prevailed. I took one, and tried to engross myself.

'Which section do you like the most in the newspaper?' She had developed a new respect for books and papers because of living with me. She climbed on my back while asking that. I could feel the bulge of her breasts on my spine.

'I like the poll of the day section. The Yes, No, Can't Say, one.'

'And what's so intriguing about these silly polls.'

'I am intrigued by the fact that there are some fools in this world who waste a rupee of theirs messaging that they "can't say." I mean, when you don't have an opinion, then why to give an opinion. How ridiculous is that.' She gave a nod.

'Yeah! Actually, they are bigger fools than my *langur*.' Priyanka had befriended a langur who lived on a tree around our house. She used to feed him and he would come back every day. I didn't like that langur, and had told her not to feed him or soon there would be many around us.

'There are so many people who are dying hungry and you rich people care for dogs and langurs. Feed a child instead of that gruesome monkey. It will be so much better. Anyways, there is food crisis in our country.'

Priyanka held someone else responsible for food shortage, 'it's the gods of this country who are to be held responsible for this food crisis my dear. See, the tea vendor spills the first cup of his day on the road, for the *gods*. A friend of mine used to throw the first few grains of rice on the floor before starting his meal, for the *gods*. The temple priest and so many other devotees waste so much food in front of those idols. And you think that there is a food shortage in our country because I am feeding these poor

Love, Lust & Lies

langurs. The *gods* are eating a lot you see. Gods are to be held responsible.' She made sense with that.

She continued, 'and if you so much want to feed people, then why don't you open a restaurant. Feed as much as you want to.' Now Priyanka grunted those lines with sarcasm, but left me with an idea to dwell upon.

'I think you are right, I must open a restaurant. So many tourists come to this place. A restaurant is a great idea.'

Actually I was quite worried those days, maybe she will ask me to fuck off the next time I pull out unfinished. After all, till when can I eat on her money. Though chances were negligible of her ever saying so. But you never know when the Mrs. Khanna in her gets up. At the end of the day, she belonged to a rich family. A snake and a rich person, both are quite the same. Can't be trusted much.

Next day, the first thing I did was to go out to the marketplace around Naini lake and see a broker. I told him my requirements of a place good enough to open a small restaurant. He took me around, and after checking out a few of them, I booked one. The view of the lake and the crowds outside were great from that room. Romeos and Juliets love to hang around at such places.

In a fortnight's time I had set it up. Eight round tables, with a plastic rose on each one of it, 3 waiters and 2 cooks. 1 slant eyed chap, obviously for cooking Chinese.

Priyanka wanted me to name the restaurant "The Priyanka's." I gave her idea a thumbs down. I wanted a Muslim name. See, all around India, people think that Muslims are hardcore non-vegetarians. And also feel that they cook some amazing non-veg stuff. Now the cook inside can be a Hindu, but if the name outside on the board is a Muslim, people will walk in.

Being politically correct to make sure that Priyanka isn't offended, I told her that I wanted to name it behind my ammi. I named it, "The Najma's." With the name I also made sure that the board had the number 786 up there. That would again help me get more business.

Soon I was in business. With the opening of the restaurant, I became a little less insecure. But still while humping Priyanka I tried to look as less in her eyes as possible. At times while knocking her, she would grab my face in her palms, keep swinging and force me to look into her eyes. Giving me a hint that she knew what was troubling me. As if playing with me. Though I was pretty sure she was not intelligent enough to know what was in my mind. That's too deep a thought in my head for anyone else to make out.

I lay down next to Priyanka once again. Not finding sleep. There was a storm brewing within me. My mind went back to the dream I was having before the squall ended it. That night the yeti; Priyanka's father, Pinocchio and Mrs. Khanna had visited me in my dreams. They had with them a band of horrifying looking black men. Like those bouncers at nightclubs. Negros, boxers. These niggers held me upside down and after stripping me naked, slapped my face, and my bum at the same time. *Chataak! Chataak!* Both, bum and face turned red in seconds.

Yeti spat on my face and barked a rhyming line, "that's position 69. Bum and face at the same time." Mrs. Khanna growled. "That's for running away with my daughter you thug." And then Pinocchio came right into my face which was upside down. Hissed, "return my money or I swear I will kill you right here and pee in your dead skull." I begged for mercy, but they got crueler. And then suddenly someone came for my rescue. The door opened. A girl's silhouette with that old "three knot three" rifle in hand walked in. I thought Priyanka was here for my rescue. Niggers looked at her. She walked closer. It was Zareen. She loaded the rifle, and Bam! Bam! Bam! She shot all of them dead. All of them who were troubling me for so long. And then with tears in her eyes she said, 'I will always be there for you, even if you were never there for me.'

I woke up and swung open the window panes allowing the robust wind to blow my face left right center. I turned and looked at Priyanka, she was sleeping peacefully and had coiled like a barbed spiky wire. Her tattoo of the dragon on the lower back, looking at me. Telling me, "Ameen, this is the same way you will burn in the hellfire for deserting Zareen. For leaving her stranded. She is waiting for you there, your *wife* is expecting you there. And you, you are such a bastard. You are such a *harami*. Having a heavenly time over here, humping this girl. And what about your parents? Don't they want you to serve them well for what all they did for you. How can you be such an asshole. How can you be living in an oblivious world? Shame on you, you jerk. Shame on you."

I became angry at myself, sorry for myself and vulnerable at the same time. How is Zareen? How is she? Is she still waiting for me? I have again used her as a sacrificial sheep. As I have on so many occasions earlier.

I can't do this. I need to go. I need to talk to her. I need to go and talk to abba-ammi. Till when can I hide this acidic truth. I can't let Zareen be like that. This coward in me needs to fuck off.

I also haven't cared much for my parents. My abba, my ammi. Last time I had called from the railway station in Bombay, ammi had said that abba's health is deteriorating. How is he? Is he fine now? I never cared. I went too deep inside Priyanka. But now I have come out. And come out for good.

I had decided to break the shackles of ignorance and get ammi-abba with me. To get Zareen with me. I don't care how Priyanka will react to that. But I am not going to make her my excuse for not giving Zareen what she deserves to get. I have lived a very slippery life, as if on a skating ring. On a skating ring it's considered good to be at the place where the puck is. You need to go to the puck and grab it. My puck was Zareen. Always has been. She had always been hammered and ditched from one corner of the ring to another. I had decided to grab her, be with her.

"Some men have thousands of reasons, why they can't do, what they want to. When all they need is one reason, why they can."

Probably I now knew that one reason why I need to be with Zareen. I figured it out quite late, but glad that I figured it out at least.

         Love, Lust & Lies

20th

Within a few days I was on the roads that lead to my town. Resolute to tell it all to my parents. All about Priyanka, all about my new life. Confess all my lies. All about my illegitimate love story. And our relation. And my hotel. And her job. And her hair, her eyes, her lips. Hoping that they will understand. Hoping that they will pardon me.

Resolute to meet Zareen. Look deep into her eyes. To apologize. To tell her that she means more to me than any other thing in my life. To tell her to come with me. Stay with me. Hoping that she will understand. Hoping that she will pardon me.

But more than these two things, I was worried about the Pinocchio episode. He must have complained about the robbery. But *am* I going to confess about this appalling act of mine as well. Are my balls big enough now to admit this as well?

NO! I will lie. I will hide this one. I am still not brave enough to admit this reprehensible act of mine. Admit that I went so deep inside Priyanka that I made a thief out of me. That is the worst part about lying. You lie once, and you have to lie over a thousand times again to hide it.

Back in Nainital, Priyanka was cribbing. She wanted to check out more places in and around Nainital. I was too much consumed in my own thoughts. In my own worries. I told her to go ahead and check them out herself. She had looked at me with a gloomy face. She knew that our little world was no more as beautiful as it used to be. Things were on the brink of falling apart. We were no more pouncing on each other as hungry animals. The fire was going lull. She didn't speak a word. Next day she packed her small haversack, left a note next to me, and left.

The note read: *"I love you. With the same madness and the same rashness as before."*

It unnerved me for a second. But I had already decided. Zareen needs to be here. No matter what Priyanka later feels or says. Abba-ammi need to be here. No matter what Priyanka later says or feels.

There was no Maruti or abba or ammi at the station to pick me up. It was all different this time. A little scared of what future holds, I stepped down, hired a cab, the roads looking a little more bumpy than usual, I reached home.

The door was open. I walked in. The old rickety chair of my abba still at its place. Only the person sitting on it was ammi, not abba. Her eyes closed. Asleep. I stood right over her shoulders, behind her, observing her hair. They had turned all white.

'*Assalam valaikum* ammi.' She slowly opened her eyes. Turned around as characters in films turn in a slo-mo. I noticed that she was no more the ammi of my childhood. She was old now. She was stunned to see me there suddenly.

'Ameen. When did you come? How have you been?' She got up from her chair, walked a couple of steps with a stoop, came forward, and hugged me.

'Where had you vanished? We were so worried. No phones, no letters.' Her voice husky. When a kid, she used to bend down to hug me. Now I had to bend in order to hug her. How time flies by. You never come to know. Time is the scariest thing. By far, the *most* scariest.

'How is abba? Where is he?' Ammi took me inside their bedroom. Abba was lying on his bed. His skull cap still intact. The pajama still in that typical fashion, showing the bump of his ankle clearly.

'He is no more mobile. He lies on his bed, looking at the ceiling all day long. He can't even walk up to the toilet. He pees and....' Ammi lost her voice after that. Abba's condition was very disturbing.

The faces of ammi-abba had wrinkles galore. The wrinkles told their story. Their whole life's journey showing on their skin clearly. I felt miserable. For not paying attention to them. For letting them be here alone all this while. For not paying enough attention when these wrinkles were drawing up one by one on their skin.

While having lunch with ammi, I asked her, 'Ammi, do you still wear that veil when you walk out of the door.'

'Nah! Who is going to look at this old lady now. And I am no more scared of your abba either. I think he is also a little less insecure now. He knows nobody will hit on me anymore.' Her face broke into a long smile.

'Ammi, can I ask you something? Do you really love abba. Were you happy to be Mrs. Jalal?' She thought over my question with her right cheek resting on her right palm. She smiled and sat back, straight, 'I will quote a line from your abba's diary which he used to read me out sometimes. It goes somewhat like this. "Love at first sight is easy to understand. It is when two people have been looking at each other for a life time, that it becomes a miracle." And trust me, no matter even if we had differences and those cold and hot wars, it has been a miracle.'

I was very glad to hear that. Later I asked, 'why don't you apply henna to your hair, ammi?'

'Where is the strength left in my bones? Let your wife come, I will make her apply some every weekend.' I blushed, she grinned, and I noticed that a few of her teeth were also gone.

I wanted to say, "ammi, my wife is just next door. I will get her to you soon." Instead I asked, 'ammi, how is Zareen?'

'She got *married*.'

That was that. I had lost her. Zareen was no more going to be mine. I had let her go. She went away. My Zareen.....

Everything looked hazy, misty. As Nainital looks from my window on a stormy night. I lost interest in my lunch. Suddenly felt too full to eat. No tears rolled down. The shock of losing Zareen was something much more. Much bigger a pain than what can be alleviated by shedding a few drops down.

'Who.... Who did she get ma....?' I asked, hiding my pain. Quite failed at that. But surprises and shocks were still many.

'To Zain. There was a huge drama and fuss at her place for several days. She refused to get married. She would cry and yell and scream that somebody is waiting for her. Her parents locked her in a room, whipped her, but she didn't say who he was. They asked her several times, when he would come. He never came. Finally was married. Do you have any idea who this guy was?'

I looked at her for a brief second. Lowered my eyes.

'No! I don't know who that *harami* was.'

Obviously that *harami* was sitting right in front of her. Zareen had done it again. She had taken it all on her. Didn't give out my name. She waited for me. She waited and waited for me. And I. I never noticed. I never *fucking* noticed. Was too busy *fucking* my college babe. Too busy shaving off my beard. Too busy talking with Americans on the Tic-Tic machine. Too busy buying jeans and steel watches. Too busy in noticing and observing every other thing except Zareen.

I got up and stormed out of my room. Kept on drifting like a lost gladiator. Eyes still dry. Mind numb. Body anesthetized. I walked towards Zain's house. Or rather, Zareen's house. A married Zareen, or rather a Zareen who had been married again.

Zain opened the door, elated.

Love, Lust & Lies

'Oh my god. Ameen. Where had you been?' He hugged me and we walked in. We sat in the drawing room. Zain was fatter than before. Was chewing tobacco now instead of smoking cigarettes.

'I tried all possible ways to get in touch with you. All my friends were here for my marriage, but you.' I forced a smile and apologized. He then called out the name of the person I desperately wanted to see.

'Zareen. Look who is here. Your old friend.' The curtain dividing the room came to life. My Zareen, now Zain's Zareen, walked in. She looked at me. I looked at her. We looked at each other.

And silence spoke a billion, zillion, squillian words. Her eyes asked. My eyes didn't have appropriate answers. Her eyes still looked at me with the same love and affection. My eyes didn't like that. My eyes wanted her eyes to curse me, to abuse me. To hate me. But they didn't. Her eyes now went wet, my eyes were already wet.

'*Arrey*, will you stand there and keep looking at him or sit and talk with your old friend. He is the only thing common between us. An old *friend* of both of us.' I noticed his stress on the word *friend*. Thought maybe he knows about our discreet marriage. But next second I rubbished the thought. Zareen will never let my name out of her mouth.

She took a seat right opposite me. Eyes no more on me. My eyes still on her. Henna still dark and clear on her hands, arms, and feet. Skin glowing as always. Hair covered with a *dupatta*.

'So where have you been all these years Ameen?'

'In Nainital.'

'*Nainital*. What were you doing in Nainital.?'

'I have opened a small restaurant out there.'

'That's good. Actually we are planning our honeymoon. I think Nainital will be a fun place to visit.' He placed his hands around Zareen. That pinched me hard. Pierced my heart.

'Yeah, come over. It's a beautiful place.' A maid walked in with a tray full of delicacies. Laid it on the table, and left. Zain prompted Zareen to serve me. She moved forward, reached for a bowl, hands shaking a bit, filled it with some *halwa* and kept it in front of me.

Telephone rang inside. Zain excused himself. It was now me and her in the room. The *halwa* tasted so dry. I somehow forced it below my throat. Took a sip of water. Looked at her once again. She was again looking at me.

'Where did you vanish? I waited....' Her throat gave up. I still had no reasonable answer.

I asked her, 'Is her caring?'

'Very.'

'Is he loving?'

'Very.'

'Are you happy?'

'Very.' I paused. And asked, 'did you miss me?' She paused. And answered, 'Very.'

And tears rolled down, our hearts sank, our hands met, our foreheads met in the middle and clapped against each other. Again and again.

'It was not written. Zareen, god had different plans for us. It's all written. *kismet,* as they say.' We cried for another minute. I got up, looked at her, 'Don't cry. Please don't.'

'I cried every night wondering how to make it right. To make this so called *kismet* right.'

'You know I don't like it. Smile. You have a million times better husband and a man than me.'

Love, Lust & Lies

I started walking out. She held my hand and hugged me, tight. I held her tight. We cried and hugged and cried. I knew she would not let me go. If Zain catches us like this, things would have become worse. Not for me, but for her. I sidled away. Turned and walked out.

By the time I reached home, ammi-abba were asleep. My head was still heavy. Dazed. I had cried all the way back. I locked myself in the toilet, and cried some more. In that dark toilet, I noticed my dark reflection in the cracked mirror. I got up, looked at my reflection for a whole minute and spat on myself. Spat and spat and spat till there was no saliva left on my tongue. I deserved every bit of that.

Next day in the morning we all were sitting in abba's room. With a lot of difficulty, he asked, 'Kashif called me a few years back. He had said that you stole a lot of money and jewelry from his house. Is that true?' As I had guessed, Pinocchio had complained. But it didn't take me by surprise. Obviously, I was prepared for this one.

With a straight face, and looking straight into his eyes, I answered, 'No. That's not true. He is lying.'

That one line and one question and one poker look on my face did it all. Convinced him enough that I was not lying. I have always been a master at this art called lying.

Later that night, I overheard ammi-abba talking over the same topic.

'Do you really believe in what Ameen said today. Was he speaking the truth?' Ammi had asked.

'Of course, he was speaking the truth. He was not lying. That Kashif was lying. He never took care of Ameen in *Bum-bayee*, what can you expect from a man like Kashif. Ameen can't commit such a shameful act. He is *my* son. *My son.*'

I always knew ammi was more intelligent between the two. I went in their room. A lantern illuminated the room that was kept in a corner.

'Ammi, abba. I want to say something.' Abba rolled his eyeballs to look at me.

'You both can come and live with me in Nainital. I am working there. You know how beautiful that place is. It will be really wonderful if we all can live together.' They both kept quiet. Abba rolled his eyeballs away. Staring now at the ceiling.

'Why don't you come and stay with us. Here, in your own town.'

'But ammi I have opened a restaurant out there. And I also have Pri.....' I stopped immediately. Then continued, 'and then how does it matter if it's our town or any other town in the whole world. What matters is that we all stay together. As a family.'

'It does matter. It's the destiny and privilege for an ice-cube to melt in its own water.' Her face was apathetic. With that I knew they won't come. I didn't push hard either. It would have been of no use.

'Anyways, you are going to visit us at regular intervals. Aren't you?'

I nodded. But was there an option.

I was leaving the next day. Back for Nainital. Our old Maruti was in shambles now. A few Honda cities and Toyota Corollas had arrived in my town. Many people were carrying a cell phone as well. My town was also changing. Slow as a tortoise, but was changing undeniably.

I called for a cab to take me to the station. I met abba, and then walked outside with ammi.

'Don't forget us like the last time. Stay in touch.' I hugged her, wiped the corners of her eyes. I didn't like it. This time I truly wanted them to come with me. But I knew they won't agree. Sometimes bidding adieu is the only solution. I sneaked into the taxi. The driver moved the keys and the car made coughing sound as always. I looked out from the window. Soon, as on so many occasions, her silhouette waving its right hand got hazy, small, small and small, and then vanish somewhere in thin air.

That was the last time I saw my ammi-abba. I didn't see them ever again.

"A winner makes commitment. A loser makes promises. You were not born a winner, and you were not born a loser. You are what you make yourself to be."

It's me and my choices that are responsible for making a loser out of me. So many hollow promises. Not a single commitment I remember. I was going back a loser. Had lost ammi-abba. Had lost Zareen. I was returning a failure.

Those winters Bombay was molested. And abused and assailed for three long torturous days. Some ten young boys, brainwashed in the name of religion, lass with assault rifles and grenades, went mad in a coordinated shooting and bombing that began on 26th November and lasted until 29th, killing at least 173 people and wounding at least 308.

The news channels, newspapers, tabloids had nothing else but 26/11 to write about. It was said to be India's 9/11. Different personalities on news channels started having debates and discussions. The topic, "why are Muslims knocking down, blowing places every other day." It became a hot topic for discussions. The debates continued for several days. I watched the burning dome of the Taj hotel alone in that cottage in Nainital. Priyanka was still not back from her trip.

She returned a day later. And I was glad that she had. I was quite missing her. This loser gladiator had only her to look forward to. Only her in which I could find some solace. A fresh beginning was on my mind again. I don't know how many times in my life I had to make a fresh beginning. But it's good in a way. One actually needs to do that. See, everything in this world, everything loses its sheen after a certain point of time. Nothing is permanent and nothing remains new. May it be a machine, an animal or a human body. Or Love, life, or lust. You regularly need to refresh it. Pep it all up. Make a fresh start instead of cribbing about your harsh past. Every time I made one, I was happier. This time it would be the last time though.

'I *too* love you with the same madness and rashness. Still,' I said the same night. 'Will you marry me?' Priyanka looked apathetically for a brief moment. Then looked a bit staggered.

'Close your eyes,' she said, and I did. For good two minutes.

'Open.' And my! She was standing in a *veil*. Covered from head to toe. Wearing a burqa.

'Now come forward and unravel me. Flip this cloth hanging lose in front of my face.' I did that. With a bit of hesitation.

'Now ask the question again.'

'Will you marry me?'

'Yes I will.' We hugged. The little small cracks that had developed got lost with that warm hug.

'By the way, how do I look in this dress?' She turned and twirled flaunting it.

'Like a black haunted figure,' I said with a tinge of sarcasm. 'Why you bought it by the way?'

'I thought this will impress you. You were constantly drifting away.' She said sleepily. 'So when I become Mrs. Jalal, will you not tell me to wear a burqa?'

'Never! You can go around in a bikini if you want to, but never in a burqa.'

We went for a walk in the woods in the dark.

'So, where did you go? What all places did you see?'

'I went to Kasauni. Got a clearer look of the Himalayas from there. Then I visited Sat Tal, and even camped at Jim Corbett for three nights.'

'Did you spot a tiger?' She shook her head.

'I know you were not in Nainital when I was on my solitary tour.' How she knows that, I thought.

'You went to your town, right.' I said a meek yes. 'I also know whom you had gone to meet.' I trembled. Did she find out about Zareen? Is she going to kill me? Yes, she is. That's why she is taking me for a walk in this dark.

'Obviously to meet your parents. I found the bus ticket in your shirt's pocket.'

Phew! That was close.

That evening it was close. For sure. But soon it was going to be much more closer.

That day a crow was cawing since morning, sitting on our window pane. I tried to shoo it away. It just didn't cave in. When a crow caws on your rooftop, they say a visitor is on its way. Never, ever, in my wildest of nightmares could I have guessed that when my door will be knocked that afternoon, it would be - *Zareen*. There was some strange bond, some ghost-thread that was not letting me move away from her I suppose.

As Zain had said, he would come to Nainital for his honeymoon. He had arrived for one. When I opened the door and found Zain and Zareen standing outside with a huge smirk on his face, I had almost fainted. Not because of his long smirk, but the very same moment I made out that today, even if Batman and the joker, and Ram and Ravana, come over in tandem for my rescue, Zareen *will* find out about Priyanka. She *will* come to know of the reason why I kept her waiting? Why I ditched her?

She will curse herself. For waiting for me. For taking all that flak from her parents, and all those tongue lashes and whip lashes. For remaining in solitary confinement while I was celebrating every day of my life with this chick. All those painful moments, all those hurtful, distressful moments of pain, in which all she did was to wait for one call of mine. Every day when the sun rose from the east, and sank in the west, she had hoped that it will get me when it rises again the next morning. The sun as usual did rise, but never ever it brought me, or my call, or my news, or any information about my whereabouts.

'Surprise! Ha-ha! Ha-ha! Ha-ha!' Zain hugged me and walked in straight. Zareen trailing him. I closed the door. Palms by now soaked in sweat.

Then Zain said, 'see, I thought about calling you before coming over. But thought that a surprise will be better. Wasn't it?' His smile now could match the width of all the oceans. "No you dumbfuck. You don't know how much a tight spot you are going to put me in," I thought and nodded at the same time.

The moment of truth. Priyanka walked in and Ameen's Zareen met Ameen's Priyanka. Till date, I don't know how she reacted when she saw Priyanka for the first time. What her eyes exclaimed, if her face muscles contracted or expanded, if she got Goosebumps? For one plain and simple reason. I didn't have balls big enough to look into her eyes.

'Hi, I am Priyanka. Ameen's fiancé. He must have told you guys about me. *Didn't he?*' Now that's stupid. Zain stood there like a plastic mannequin at those big malls. And then a thin smile graced his face.

'Oye! You have a fiancé and never told us. Girlfriend!' I looked at the ground and then outside at the langurs, and then at Priyanka, and then somewhere else, but Zareen.

'Congratulations brother.' He came forward and hugged me tight. I felt like crushing him the same way. 'By the way, I am Zain, and this is my wife Zareen.'

'Oh, so you guys are Zain and Zareen. Ameen would talk day in and day out about you guys. My god. Today I am going to grill you guys and ask all about his childhood.'

Priyanka took them inside the other room, while I gave an excuse of a call to make. Pretending of an imaginary call at the other end, I kept on holding the receiver to my ear, while noises of Ha-Ha, Ho-Ho kept traveling out persistently from that room.

The disturbing element was, noises were only of two people. Zain and Priyanka.

I stood there with the receiver all the time to my ears. My eyes all the time at the door which led to the other room. Petrified of even thinking about entering that room. Priyanka and Zain called out several times for me, but I didn't make a move.

'Learn to tackle pressure Ameen. You must divide your time equally between work and family. Ask Zareen. I never talk about work at home. Right Zareen.' Zain shouted from inside.

I could hear Zain narrating the Rohan incidence and then the umbrella flicking days. Once they were done with that episode, and laughed like hooligans, Priyanka had asked Zareen to share some experiences. She narrated the Bakri-eid incident, when I used to feed my goat the greenest of the grass and let her goat starve. She narrated the incidence when we ran to the theater and she was abused. Then many more. I was unable to make myself listen more. I broke down. Cried silently with that receiver to my ear.

After about an hour when they got up to leave, I threw the receiver down. I apologized for being busy all the while. Lead them outside, greeted them and watched them go with a heavy heart. I had still not managed to look into Zareen's eyes. Was she enraged? Was she sulking? Was she sad, broken, shattered? I didn't know. But I came to know soon.

For next day, early in the morning someone knocked at the door. Half asleep, I opened it, shocked to see Zareen standing outside. Alone.

'I want to talk to you. Can you come for a walk with me.' I peeped inside. Priyanka was still fast asleep. I quietly walked out, closing the door slowly behind me.

Love, Lust & Lies

We were walking down the hill. It was still foggy. I noticed her hair, all tousled, she looked in a pathetic shape. As if, just returned from some war. Goes without a saying, she was the one who was doing all the talking.

'Congratulations. You got engaged.' I didn't speak. 'Congratulations for becoming the light of someone else's eyes. For becoming the oxygen of someone else's life.' I didn't dare to speak. What could have I?

'I don't hold you responsible for anything. Our story was written like this. As you used to say, it's all written. *Kismet*. We feel that we are the writers of our books, and we think we know how we are going to end it. But the truth is, we don't.'

Grief and guilt was tearing my heart. We walked a little more, and then she said, 'It's time to become strangers once again. I guess, that is the only way out.' I didn't like that. I forced myself to speak up.

'Become strangers once again. I don't know how that is possible.' I looked at her. Her eyes still brimming with tears and love for me.

She continued, 'I don't know how, but that's the only possible way out. Or else, till when can I handle my words trembling with your heartbeat. The disgraces of my past are my constant companions. And you too are possessed by the old memories.' I had no answers to this one.

She then held my hand as had done so many times in our younger days, and said, 'It looks like our love story is going to be incomplete. It has been cut short.' She held my face with her warm palms, 'But we still can end it in a beautiful way.'

She sidled closer, and kissed me. I turned my face away. 'The taste of the first kiss always remains on your lips. Your taste is still fresh on my lips.' A few meters away, was a small derelict cottage.

'Can we go in there and.....' She didn't complete it. Incomplete sentences and lines can be very seducing. There is a mysterious charm in them. She held my index finger, and lead me into that ramshackle. I followed like a puppy.

She opened the door of the cottage, dust unsettled, and then settled on our faces. She wiped her face, and then my face. We walked in. She closed the door. Our eyes took their own sweet time to adjust to the darkness of the room. I looked at her apathetically. No idea how should I react. She looked at me with a lot of love. Rammed me back on the wall. Kissed my lips again.

'Ah! I was so correct. Your lips taste the same. I can never forget this taste of yours.' She moved a few steps back and unclipped her hair. They flew down regally. She came closer. Her hands went at her back. I could see she was breathing heavily. Her heart was pounding. My condition was no different.

'You know what, losing the person you love hurts. Some people say you will get over it easily. But it's really tough. Especially when the one you love is the only one you loved.' She stopped for a brief second, and then said, 'but I will manage.' She held my gaze with hers.

'This place looks great to have sex.' She moved a step closer, brought her face right in my face, 'but you know what, any place that is great to have sex, is also great to kill somebody.'

'What?' I squeaked like a rat.

She brought her hands in front. Zareen had a silver kukri in her hands. Her gaze fixed, target set, and then in a flash, before I could make out anything, Zareen had placed it deep inside my throat. Zareen had written the last pages of my book just then. In red ink.

My knees shook badly, gave up, and I slipped down. My eyes begging her to pull this thing out, a fountain of blood sprawling all around. Zareen walked away from me. Opened the door, moved out, took a roundabout turn, her two hands stretched, holding the door, as if imitating Jesus on a cross. Her silhouette stood there gazing at my dying body, I don't know exactly if that was a dewdrop or a tear on the cheeks of her silhouette, for she slammed the door close the next moment. But if I had to bet, I would say that it was a dewdrop.

Locked in this dark dungeon, with a sharp kukri in my neck, my throat slashed, blood dripping, my legs flicking, going berserk. Up-down, up-down. Right-left, left-right. Throwing themselves everywhere. Eyes popping out. My state was exactly like a freshly slaughtered goat on a Bakri-Eid morning.

I was dying. Very Slowly, at a snail's pace, like the python was guzzling the fat mouse that summer evening at the Corbett park.

And I was extremely worried. Not about myself or my slashed throat. That worry was last on the list. I was worried for my ammi...........

I lay there like that, reading the pages of my life. My blood on the floor, all around, now freezing due to cold. Pretty sure that this ramshackle was destined to be the place where I would breathe my last breath. Abba used to comment, "Nainital is a place where you can live and die peacefully, gladly, contentedly. The crisp and fresh breeze of this valley will take you straight to the doorsteps of jannat." If his words were for real, then I am going there in no time.

But the door swung open again. My squinted eyes, not registering clearly now. It was all obscure, cloudy. But I could see a fat woman and a thin man. The man was wearing a skull cap like my abba, and a kurta pajama. They spotted me on the floor, realized that I was dying. They shrieked, shouted. From their conversation I could make out that they heard some noises and rushed to this cottage.

They picked me up; the man held my legs and the woman somehow managed to hold me from my shoulders. My body was hanging like a heavy mattress between them. They were carrying me out of that dilapidated cottage. They were constantly shouting. They took me to another cottage, a few meters away.

The condition of this cottage was worse. A few more people were shouting. They all were standing around a woman who was lying on a wicker mat. That woman in the center was also shouting. That woman was giving birth to a child.

Do you know how a child is born? The mother shouts and shouts and shouts till her throat gives up. But you know what, in such situations, the *throat* never gives up. She keeps on shouting. The people around are no less. They shout louder than her; "push, push, harder, harder."

"Ameen, you created a lot of trouble and pain for me at the time of your birth. Yours was not an easy birth." I remember ammi telling me.

Finally after a lot of hard work and pains a child was born. Every other person stopped shouting. Nobody had energy even to hum. And then the child cried, announcing to the whole world that he had arrived. He shouted and cried and yelled and screamed.

232   Love, Lust & Lies

Ten meters away a boy was born, life was about to begin, and here my life was on the verge of getting over.

When that newborn's innocent shrieks enthralled that room for the first time, I closed my eyes, for one last time.

Some...times....I feel.... that it's all written.... Kismet...As they say.

Priyanka

Till date I don't know who did it. Nor I want to find it out. How will it make a difference. He is gone. Never to return. It was a hard truth to digest. Life looked gloomy and miserable after that. Our ramshackle was looking way too big for me. It would run to eat me up. I bought another small place.

I didn't sell that old little heaven of ours. It's still there. Whenever I miss him, I go and sit there and cry there, and try and feel him there.

I got in touch with my parents. Mom was very happy. But I still live in Nainital. Write articles and columns, and that restaurant is also there. I send some money over to his parents. He always worried about them.

But with time, everything gets better. Time is the best medicine. The best healer. I will also move on. May be will find some other man as well. But nobody will be able to replace him.

On days I visit his grave with a bouquet of fresh flowers. The whole town goes abuzz that a Hindu girl visits a Muslim man's grave. I overhear people who whisper that how can I dress in a jeans and a T-shirt on my visit to a graveyard. And not in a burqa. I could have donned a burqa. But he would not have liked it. He will be happy to see me free as a bird.

I lost a part of mine with him. A voidness has developed. A strange emptiness. I guess it will take hell lot of a time. Trust me, hell lot of a time to move on completely.

Zareen

The moment I decided to do it, I had shivered at the idea. But I had taken a decision, and I had to kill him no matter what. It all happened so quickly. In haste. But I don't regret it.

I do feel guilty, but content now. Somewhat guilt-pleasure kind of a feeling. I miss him. But even if he had been alive I would have missed him the same. And I would have found it really hard to move on knowing that he is sleeping peacefully with his hands around some other girl.

I had waited all my life. Cried all my life for him. But when I came to know about Priyanka, I didn't cry. I had taken decision somewhere then. Probably Ameen could have made out my intentions had he seen straight in my eyes the day I had visited him. But he didn't. He didn't have balls to do that.

I was a bit finicky, if I would really be able to pierce his throat or not. If I would generate enough power in my hands when the moment arrives. But then, I did the same what Ameen did all his life with me. I lied to him.

When I took him for what was going to be his last walk, I had said that I still love him. But by then, all my love for him had turned into deep hatred. He fell for my lie. And for the first time I realized that a lie can do wonders for you.

All I want to say is, Thank you Ameen. For making me hate you so much. And for making me learn the importance of this great art called lying. As you used to say, street smarts are smarter than book smarts. See, I just now proved you right. Didn't I learn the tricks well from you? I am sure you will agree. Nevertheless, I still love you.

You know I do. I always have. Haven't I?

I am glad that if it had to be somebody, then it was Zareen. For I, someday had to pay for my innumerous lies. Who else deserved to punish me more but Zareen. All my life I lied to her. Lied without caring that every minute, every second she was waiting, dying in trepidation. Lied without caring for her feelings and emotions. Without caring for her affection and her concern. Her regard, her sentiments, and her love. Who else deserved to punish me more but Zareen.

And for all the lies to my abba-ammi. Lies to Priyanka. Lies to those American customers. Lies to Pinocchio. Lies to so many others I came across in my life. In fact I even dared to lie to the almighty. See, I promised to get my beard back. Never ever did I care enough for it later.

Probably the seeds of lying were laid in me young. When I heard that crow's story. The way he lied to attain his freedom. I wanted to learn the art of lying in order to create a lie, a rescue plan, which could free my ammi of the haunted life she was leading under that black robe. But somewhere down the line, I lost track. I started lying with every other possible opportunity. I became a master liar. A master at hoodwinking. Father of liars. I can call myself *"The Pop Of Liars."*

They say that there are seven sins. Gluttony, Pride, Lust, Sloth, Envy, Greed and Wrath. But they forgot to mention the biggest and the most heinous of all the sins. *Lying.* There can be no bigger crime than that. Trust me. I am speaking out of experience. Lying in this grave of mine somewhere in Nainital, I have figured this out.

I think instead of becoming a thief, I should have tried philosophy. I could have preached people how to lie and would have ended up making shit-load of money. I have decided. Next life. Philosopher. You make a lot of money. Those sadhus and babas have property worth thousands of crores. But everyone in India feels that these naked babas are some saints, or reincarnation of some god.

But let me tell you the secret cause of my death. The secret is, I became an *emotional fool*. Just for once in my life, and it was my doom. Let me explain.

India is a country full of emotional fools. And all the corrupted ministers born in this land, biggest of the scums, biggest of the villains, know this very well. Making us fight in the name of religion, cast, creed. Eating our taxes, procrastinating their promises, every inch of their body smelling of corruption, sucking the poor man's blood, yet, ending up winning elections after elections. That's the trick of making big in this land. All the successful men out here, each and every one of them, may it be a politician or those babas and sadhus. They are neither emotional, nor fools. They all pretend to be emotional. And that is why they are successful. They all follow the same policy.

Be as big a bastard you want to be, but never reveal your true colors. You may end up ruling this country.

See, I am no Nehru or Gandhi to tell you all this. But trust me, what I realized now is, Gandhi-Nehru probably figured out much earlier that Indians are emotional fools.

And that is also the cause of my death. I was never an emotional guy. Never! I was doing well. Lying and making merry as always. Always carrying out pretence. But I became emotional when it came to Zareen. That last afternoon of my life, we switched roles. She was lying, and I emotionally followed, and see what happened. I was murdered. I was killed. She learnt well from me. She always did. See, these illiterate people may not know how to read and write, but they are great at observing and learning. Oh Zareen, you just now proved me right that street smarts are way clever than book smarts.

Every romantic hero meets the same fate. All the Romeos and Majnus ended dead. They all were such losers. Emotional fools. Practical people are successful. Be practical. Not emotional. Being emotional makes you rigid. Don't be. It never helps. Though all the books and all the great men of this country will tell you and preach you to be emotional. Trash them and their quotations. Be practical.

See that is why these western countries are so developed. They are a bunch of practical people. They will attack any country on this planet without caring for the innumerous lives they are going to take. They don't have any emotions whatsoever. You rub them the wrong way, and the very next minute their President will announce, "We are at *war*."

Though we need to be thankful to them in some incongruous way. They are the ones who are responsible for uniting us. Look at our history closely. In how many constituencies were we broken. Nizams, Marathas, Mughals, Rajputs. We were so divided. They were the ones who united us. And we crib that it was the British who divided us. Hell no!

Were we kids in 1947. Why didn't we use our own fucking heads. We turn into hypocrites and try and conceal the great dividing mistake we committed by saying that it was the British who divided us. But the reason to worry is, that we still haven't learnt from that mistake of ours.

On days, Priyanka visits my grave with a bouquet of flowers. And the whole valley of Nainital goes abuzz with news that a Hindu girl visits a Muslim man's grave. There are many more such discriminations which are stunting our country's growth. Acting as barriers and hurdles.

We are not united. We were not united and god knows what future holds. It looks grim. Hollow. No matter how much we may shout from our roof tops slogans like, "India Rising, India Shining." I don't see any rise and shine, except for our constant rise in population and kids shining boots at the railway stations.

We keep on shouting that we are secular, we are united. Cultural harmony is practiced in this land called India. Lies! All lies. India as a country is lying. Lying constantly to herself. Lying and dying constantly.

We divide on the name of religion. We divide on the name of caste and creed. We give hell lot of importance to sex and divide even on the basis of sexuality. We divide on the basis of every silly possible thing.

We beat poor taxi drivers and break their carriages with hockey sticks because the driver is from some other part of this country. The fact that he is an Indian hardly matters. That's secondary.

Sometimes I feel it will be so better if we divide this country into 50 *different* countries. Make a separate Maharashtra, make a separate Uttar Pradesh, a separate Naxal Pradesh, a separate Gurkha land. *Get lost!* Nobody cares for a proper India. Nobody sees an Indian dream. What's the use? Where's the point? Why the hell should the poor man lose his life and property just to make sure that we remain one secular country in the eyes of the world.

What all have we, India and Indians as a country achieved? Now whenever this question is asked, most of us pompously announce-:

We discovered the number zero.
We won the 1983 cricket world cup.
We are the IT hub and center for global attention these days.

We are the world's largest democracy, and also have the world's largest railway network.

Wow! Applause people.

We don't have electricity, we don't have water supply, we don't have enough food for our citizens, we don't have enough schools, we don't have enough teachers, we don't have enough hospitals, we don't have enough doctors, we don't have a fair and a fast judicial system, there are still villages where woman are scared to get out of their homes as they don't have a single piece of clothe to cover their bodies, we don't have educated respected ministers, we don't have roads, we don't have tolerance against women, we don't have enough jobs, in fact we even don't have enough condoms so that our men can produce a little less than what they are producing. We don't have anything, yet we are proud of giving the world a zero. Huh!

Let the white tourists visit the places I have advised them to. Let them eat their lunch and dinner in those restaurants. I will not be surprised if they will go back saying that India as a country is nothing but a butt of ridicule than an object of awe.

We need to pull up our socks quick. With less than a decade to go the dream of becoming a superpower by 2020, a dream that has been ignited in our hearts and minds by the great Abdul Kalam looks very difficult to achieve. Dreaming alone is not good enough. What is required from here on is action. And a few statesmen and no more politicians. There is a lot of difference between the two. A statesman thinks about the people, a politician thinks about the next election. While we have herds of politicos, we hardly have statesmen. We need to learn from our own gory mistakes. Need to do away with this mob mentality and dividing and segregating our own country. We need to inspire and

Love, Lust & Lies

re-inspire ourselves. But to be honest we no more need to look at the west for inspiration. They have nothing great left to teach us. The white man has become rich and completely debauched. Look at the yellow man instead. Learn from them. May it be Olympics, freedom, economy, national security. The yellow man can teach us hell of a lot.

I am not proud of my country. And let that sound blunt and awful. I don't like my country. With my own countrymen everyday dying because of hunger, because of maltreatment, how can I say that I am proud of my country. No. I am not. I don't like the current situation we are in. You either need to be ignorant or illiterate to shout and say that you are *very* proud of this country. No I am not. And I got the balls to say it in front of you all. I can't be a hypocrite like those ministers.

But you know what, *I am dying to be proud of this land.* The land from which I came. My land. India. See dead are so dumb, they just can't fucking move their ass. Even if I try to, I can't move. I am dead.

Lying in my grave I can do nothing now. But you, you I shared my life with, can possibly do hell of a lot. See, there is nothing new I can tell you, what you need to do or what you should do to make this country, *our* country a better country. We keep hearing this always. In fact we also know what should be done. But that word, 'initiative,' that is what we are scared of. You are alive and healthy. Move your fat ass and do something. Take an initiative. Contribute. No, it will not make your life boring or sad. Trust me. As Michael Jackson crooned, "if you want to make a change, start with the *"man in the mirror."*

Oh god, I am so glad I am dead. I can meet Michael now. And also my old friend. Haider. I know he has reserved the best bed in heaven's dormitory for me already. Yup Haider. I am coming. Just a minute more. A few lines just scooped in my mind.

Well, I am also glad that at least I am lucky enough that I have been laid to rest in my own country. There are many who didn't get this honorable privilege as well. Like the Mughal emperor, Bahadur Shah Zafar. Incarcerated by the British, in a dungeon in Burma, Zafar wrote these lines on the walls:

"The days of life are over, It's evening of death,
Now I can sleep without any stress in my tomb.
(But) how unlucky is Zafar! For burial
Even two yards of land were not to be had, in the land (of the)
beloved."

It's time to meet my angels now. Who will decide my fate. Heaven or hell. *Paradiso or inferno.* As abba said, if you speak truth, and follow the laws of Islam, you can get a whole Nainital exclusively for you. A Nainital of my own. Wow! The thought alone gives me gooseberry pimples. Though it looks like I am not going to get it. I lied all my life and I duped people. But somewhere I feel, I will still make it. Though I am dead, I am yet the same man. Ameen Jalal, the pop of liars. I am pretty confident that I will successfully lie to that angel god. I just now realized that next life, along with philosophy, I can also be a politician. An Indian politician. I am so good at lying you see. Ha!

Now no more one liners from the golden diary. I don't believe in them anymore. Don't waste your time reading those quotes by so called great men. They are so unrealistic. They are so *yesterday.* Use your own head instead. But I can understand, poor baby, it must be a habit of yours of reading one at the end. You can take one of my own.

"Life is a lie. A white lie. An illusion. A mirage. In the end, you get nothing. You go back empty handed. Completely stripped. Naked!"

Let me end it like those rich spoilt brats end their messages on face book. They say *cheers*. I would also say that. Cheers!

Now I feel like a rich bastard.
Dead. For sure. But rich.

AMEEN JALAL
('pop' of liars)
May *my* soul rest in peace!

Acknowledgments

A small army of people I would like to thank. They have nothing to do with the writing of the book, but they are the ones who kept the writer in me going.

Ashish Raikar. Before anyone else. For he was the one who was always there for me whenever I required any kind of advise.

My mates from the Scindia school above anyone else. Here are a few of them.

Sambhav, Bajaj, Ayush, Seengal, Saboo, Nagdev, Yadav, Dhingra, Juneja, Chajjer, Varun, Rana, Anand, Triple S, Pratik Shekhar, Bakshi, Ankur Kumar, Shantanu Pandey, Vaibhav, Dutta, Rathi, Sameer Khan, Kamboj, Harsh Preet, Rohit, Khurana, Assy, Nahata and Bangar.

Especially Kirti Azad, Vijit Goel, Jayesh Mangalam, Modi, Addy, Ritesh. And of course, Mr. Shahbaz Qaiyum.

The D.X. gang of H.R. College. Though we did split before we could have done all we had planned for, it was great to be with you guys. - Nitesh, Sanjay, Salman, Mujtaba, Zeeshan, Bela. Also Harsh and Samrath.

My Goa Gang of Boys-: Abhishek, Nitin, Rahul and Altaaf sahab.

My thanks are also due to- Jason and Sabrina Rebello, Aditya and Sneha, Adnan Aslam, Jacqueline and Shalini for reading the book chapter after chapter and suggesting me some wonderful ideas. Especially Adnan and Shalini.

The black Magic team - Abhijit, Farhat, and Sasha. Also Kaustubh, dude, your photography rocks.

I can also not forget the people who shared the room with me and tolerated me in that ramshackle we stayed in: Shekhar Koditkar, Sachin, Rahul, Vinay Bhai, Abhishek, Falgun, Rahul Sharma, Vinayak, Anup, Pradeep, Ankur Thakkar, Vijay Chauhan, Rohit and Rahul Tandon.

It was fun staying with you guys. And Tandon, thank you for allowing me to keep the lights on through the night. You know I am an owl.

Mr. Abhijit Bhaduri, an acclaimed writer himself, for guiding me and boosting my confidence.

Also thanks are due to Dr. Indu Shahani, principal, H.R. college and honorable sheriff of Mumbai. Dr. Rekha Bahadur, whose wit was never ending and her humor made me smile. Though I never thanked them personally, this is my chance to do it.

It will be incomplete without thanking my teachers at The Scindia school. Mr. V.S. Saxena for making me what I am. Mrs. Ahilya Shinde, Mr. Alok Virmani, Mr. Mridul Verma, Mr Aslam, Mrs. Aslam, Mrs. Yashodha Mukherjee, Mr. Atul Bhatt, Mr. Manoj Mishra, Dr. Bhakuni, Mrs. Madhu Tiwary.
The whole Allied Street for there never ending support and love.

All my aunties, mamu-mumanis and cousins. Especially Arshad Khaalu.
Especially Zoheb Bhai for being one of the most patient brothers I have.
Shahan Bhai for being one of the most generous brothers I have. And Naima bhabhi.
Zeeshan bhai and Zeba bhabhi,
Zain, Sheezan and Zia.
Farhan & Sunny bhai. Zeenie aapa and Sajid bhai. And also Zoya.
Also Shehla mumani & Jamshed Mamu. Ishrat mamu, Shiraz & Shayan.
Zaid, Obaid, Uzair, Arsalan and the very beautiful Nishu aapaa.
How can I forget Zaid & Saad Ahsan. You guys are great buddies.

But the list will not be complete without thanking Mr. Mushtaq Shiekh. Sir, its because of your belief and trust in me that I call myself a writer. Whatever I have learnt is from you. Your ability to make people laugh is the most admirable. Sitting in that Barista with you, always have been a pleasure.

And of course, Mandar kokate. For trusting me and my book.

And last but not the least, Almighty Allah for giving me some brains and lots of confidence.
Thank you and all the best everybody!

Azhan Ahsan
(The latest genius on the block)

Love, Lust & Lies

If anyone of the readers is interested in publishing a book with Expression publication then he/she is welcome.

For further details, visit our website -

www.expressionpublications.com.

OR MAIL US AT

E-mail id- expressionpublications@yahoo.co.in

YOU CAN ALSO MAIL THE FEEDBACK OF THIS BOOK TO OUR EDITORIAL TEAM.

E-mail id- expressionpublications@yahoo.co.in

OTHER BOOKS BY OUR PUBLICATION.

A NATIONAL BEST SELLER.

Oh shit, not again!

By

Mandar Kokate.

A MUST READ.

S/School/916/1/10